I00
FAVOURITE
SCOTTISH
POEMS

Includes BBC Radio Scotland's Listeners' Selection

EDITED BY STEWART CONN

EDINBURGH

First published in 2006 by

Luath Press Ltd
543/2 Castlehill
The Royal Mile
Edinburgh EH1 2ND
www.luath.co.uk

and

Scottish Poetry Library
5 Crichton's Close
Canongate
Edinburgh EH8 8DT
www.spl.org.uk

ISBN (10): 1-905222-61-0
ISBN (13): 978-1-9-0522261-2

The publishers acknowledge the support of

 Scottish **Arts** Council

towards the publication of this volume.

Typeset in ITC Charter and Gill Sans

Printed and bound by
Bell & Bain Ltd., Glasgow

CONTENTS

Poems marked with an asterisk are those selected by BBC Scotland listeners as their favourite Scottish poems.

Notes

ACKNOWLEDGEMENTS

Our thanks are due to the following authors, publishers and estates who have generously given permission to reproduce poems:

James Aitchison, 'House with Poplar Trees' from *Sounds Before Sleep* (Hogarth Press, 1971), reprinted by permission of the author; Marion Angus, 'Mary's Song' from *The Singin Lass* (Polygon, 2006), reprinted by permission of Birlinn Ltd; Sheena Blackhall, 'The Spik o' the Lan' from *The Spik o' the Lan* (Rainbow Publishing, 1986), reprinted by permission of the author; George Mackay Brown, 'Beachcomber' from *Collected Poems* (John Murray, 2005), reprinted by permission of Archie Bevan and of the publisher; Hamish Brown, 'Counting Sheep' from *Time Gentlemen* (Aberdeen University Press, 1983) reprinted by permission of the publisher; George Bruce, 'Departure and departure and...' from *Today Tomorrow; collected poems 1933-2000* (Polygon, 2001), reprinted by permission of the Estate of George Bruce; Tom Buchan, 'Glasgow Sabbath' from *Poems 1969-1972* (The Poni Press, 1972); John Burnside, 'Tundra's Edge' from *The Hoop* (Carcanet Press, 1988), reprinted by permission of the publisher; Elizabeth Burns, 'The Stranger' from *The Gift of Light* (diehard, 1999), reprinted by permission of the author; Ron Butlin, 'At Linton Kirk' from *Without a Backward Glance: new & selected poems* (Barzan, 2005), reprinted by permission of the author; John M. Caie, 'The Puddock' from *The Kindly North: Verse in Scots and English* (D. Wylie & Son, 1934); Angus Calder, 'Haymarket Sunset' from *Colours of Grief* (Shoestring Press, 2002), reprinted by permission of the author; Gerry Cambridge, 'A Winter Morning' from *Madame Fifi's Farewell* (Luath, 2003), reprinted by permission of the publisher; Jim Carruth, 'The man who wanted to hug cows' from *Bovine Pastoral* (Ludovic Press, 2004), reprinted by permission of the publisher; Kate Clanchy, 'Timetable' from *Slattern* (Chatto & Windus, 1995), reprinted by permission of Macmillan Publishers Ltd; W.D. Cocker, 'The Deluge' from *Poems Scots and English* (Brown, Son & Ferguson, Ltd., 1932), reprinted by permission of the publisher; Joe Corrie, 'Scottish Pride' from *Plays, Poems and Theatre Writings* (7:84 Publications, 1985), reprinted by permission of Morag Corrie; Robert Crawford, 'Scotch Broth' from *Selected Poems* (Jonathan Cape, 2005), reprinted by permission of The Random House Group Ltd; Anna Crowe, 'Gollop's' from *A Secret History of Rhubarb* (Mariscat, 2004), reprinted by permission of the author; Christine De Luca, 'A joy ta behold' from *Parallel Worlds* (Luath, 2005), reprinted by permission of the publisher; Carol Ann Duffy, 'Warming her Pearls' from *Selling Manhattan* (Anvil Press Poetry, 1987), reprinted by permission of the publisher; Douglas Dunn, 'Landscape with One Figure' from *New Selected Poems 1964-2000* (Faber & Faber, 2003), reprinted by permission of the publisher; Gillian K. Ferguson, 'Baby in the Daffodils' from *Baby* (Canongate, 2000) reprinted by permission of the author; Alison Flett, 'Lernin' from *Whit Lassyz ur Inty* (Thirsty Books, 2004), reprinted by permission of Argyll Publishing; Robert Garioch, 'Did ye see me?' from *Collected Poems* (Polygon, 2004), reprinted by permission of Birlinn Ltd; Valerie Gillies, 'Young Harper' from *The Chanter's Tune* (Canongate, 1990), reprinted by permission of the author; John Glenday, 'A Fairy Tale' from the *London Review of Books* (31 October 2002), reprinted by permission of the author; W.S. Graham, 'To Alexander Graham' from *New Collected Poems* (Faber & Faber, 2004), reprinted by permission of Michael and Margaret Snow; Alexander Gray, 'On a Cat, Ageing' from *Gossip: a book of new poems* (Porpoise Press, 1928), reprinted by permission of John Gray; Andrew Greig, 'A Small White Dog' from *Into You* (Bloodaxe Books, 2001), reprinted by permission of the publisher; Margaret Hamilton, 'Lament for a Lost Dinner Ticket' from *Noise and Smoky Breath*, ed. Hamish Whyte (Third Eye Centre/Glasgow District Libraries Publications Board, 1983), reprinted by permission of Nora Hunter; George Campbell Hay, 'The Old Fisherman' from *Collected Poems and Songs of George Campbell Hay* (Edinburgh University Press, 2000), reprinted by permission of The W.L. Lorimer Trust; Hamish Henderson, 'The Freedom Come-All-Ye' from *Collected Poems and Songs* (Curly Snake Publishing, 2000), reprinted by permission of the Estate of Hamish Henderson; Diana Hendry, 'Application' from *Handfast: Scottish poems for weddings and affimations*, ed. Lizzie MacGregor (Scottish Poetry Library/ Polygon, 2004), reprinted by permission of the author; W.N. Herbert, 'The Land o' Cakes' from *Forked Tongue* (Bloodaxe Books, 1994), reprinted by permission of the publisher; Violet Jacob, 'The Wild Geese' from *Voices from their Ain Countrie: the poems of Marion Angus and Violet Jacob* (Association for Scottish Literary Studies, 2006), reprinted by permission of Malcolm U. L. Hutton; Kathleen Jamie, 'The Queen of Sheba' from *Mr & Mrs Scotland Are Dead* (Bloodaxe Books, 2004), reprinted by permission of the publisher; Brian Johnstone, 'Behind Your Eyes' from *Homing* (Lobby Press, 2004), reprinted by permission of the author; Jackie Kay, 'In my Country' from *Other Lovers* (Bloodaxe Books, 1993), reprinted by permission of the publisher; Norman Kreitman, 'The Fly-tier's Dream' from *The Dark Horse* no. 17 (Summer 2005), reprinted by permission of the author; Joseph Lee, 'The Mother' from *Ballads of Battle* (John Murray, 1916), reprinted courtesy of University of Dundee Archive Services; Tom Leonard, 'The Voyeur' from *Intimate Voices: poems 1965-1983* (Etruscan Books, 2003), reprinted by permission of the author; Liz Lochhead, 'View of Scotland/Love Poem' from *The Colour of Black and White: poems 1984-2003* (Polygon, 2003), reprinted by permission of Birlinn Ltd; Brian McCabe, 'Seagull' from *Body Parts* (Canongate, 1999), reprinted by permission of the publisher; Norman MacCaig, 'Aunt Julia' from *The Poems of Norman MacCaig* (Polygon, 2005), reprinted by permission of Birlinn Ltd; Hugh MacDiarmid, 'The Watergaw' from *Complete Poems* vol. 1 (Carcanet Press, 1993), reprinted by permission of the publisher; Ian McDonough, 'A Night in Stoer Lighthouse' from *Clan McHine* (Chapman, 2002), reprinted by permission of the author; James McGonigal, 'The Eye of the Beholder' from *Love for Love*, eds John Burnside & Alec Finlay (pocketbooks, 2000), reprinted by permission of the author; Alasdair Maclean, 'At the Peats' from *From the Wilderness* (Victor Gollancz, 1973), reprinted by permission of David Higham Associates; Sorley MacLean, 'Hallaig' from *O Choille gu Bearradh / From Wood to Ridge* (Carcanet Press/ Birlinn, 1999), reprinted by permission of Carcanet Press; Adam McNaughton, 'The Jeelie Piece Song', from *The Edinburgh Book of Twentieth Century Scottish Poetry* (Edinburgh University Press, 2005), reprinted by permission of the author; Angela McSeveney, 'Hats', reprinted by permission of the author; Gerald Mangan, 'Ailsa Craig' from *Waiting for the Storm* (Bloodaxe Books, 1990), reprinted by permission of the publisher; Edwin Morgan, 'Canedolia' from *Collected Poems* (Carcanet Press, 1996), reprinted by permission of the publisher; Edwin Muir, 'Childhood' from *Collected Poems*

(Faber & Faber, 1960), reprinted by permission of the publisher; Stephen Mulrine, 'The Coming of the Wee Malkies' from *Poems* (Akros, 1971), reprinted by permission of the author; Charles Murray, 'Gin I Was God' from *Hamewith: the complete poems of Charles Murray* (Aberdeen University Press, 1979), reprinted courtesy of the Charles Murray Memorial Fund; Helena Nelson, 'Cake' from *Starlight on Water* (The Rialto, 2003), reprinted by permission of the publisher; Donny O'Rourke, 'Milk' from *The Waistband and other poems* (Polygon, 1997) reprinted by permission of Birlinn Ltd; Janet Paisley, 'Sarah: Fed Up' from *Ye Cannae Win* (Chapman, 2000), reprinted by permission of the publisher; Don Paterson, 'The Chartres of Gowrie' from *God's Gift to Women* (Faber & Faber, 1997), reprinted by permission of the publisher; Tom Pow, 'Crabs: Tiree' from *Landscapes and Legacies* (iynx publishing, 2003), reprinted by permission of the author; Richard Price, 'The world is busy, Katie' from *Lucky Day* (Carcanet Press, 2005), reprinted by permission of the publisher; John Purser, 'Columba to God', reprinted by permission of the author; Tessa Ransford, 'A Scented Garden' from *Medusa Dozen and other poems* (Ramsay Head Press, 1994), reprinted by permission of the author; Robert Rendall, 'Cragsman's Widow' from *Orkney Variants and other poems* (Kirkwall Press, 1951), reprinted by permission of Robert P. Rendall; Alastair Reid, 'Scotland', from *Weathering* (Canongate Books, 1981), reprinted by permission of the author; James Robertson, 'A Manifesto for MSPs' from *Voyage of Intent* (strangefruit, Scottish Book Trust/Luath, 2005), reprinted by permission of the author; Dilys Rose, 'The Maid's Room' from *Lure* (Chapman, 2003), reprinted by permission of the publisher; Iain Crichton Smith, 'Luss Village' from *Collected Poems* (Carcanet Press, 1995), reprinted by permission of the publisher; Nancy Somerville, 'The Big Hooley' from *'A New Beginning: Poems for the Turn of the Century'* (Brown & Whittaker Publishing, 1999), reprinted by permission of the author; William Soutar, 'The Tryst' from *Into a Room: selected poems of William Soutar* (Argyll, 2000), reprinted courtesy of the Trustees of the National Library of Scotland; Muriel Spark, 'Hats' from *All the Poems* (Carcanet Press, 2004), reprinted by permission of David Higham Associates; Alan Spence, 'Song' from *Glasgow Zen* (Glasgow Print Studio Press, 1981), reprinted by permission of the author; Lewis Spence, 'Capernaum' from *Collected Poems* (Serif Books, 1953); Hamish Whyte, 'Appointment' from *Handfast; Scottish poems for weddings and affimations*, ed. Lizzie MacGregor (Scottish Poetry Library/Polygon, 2004), reprinted by permission of the author; Jim C. Wilson, 'Intérieur jaune et bleu' from *The Dark Horse* no. 11 (Spring 2001), reprinted by permission of the author; Andrew Young, 'The Shepherd's Hut' from *Selected Poems* (Carcanet Press, 1998), reprinted by permission of the publisher.

Every effort has been made to trace the copyright holders of poems published in this book. If any material has been included without the appropriate acknowledgement, the publishers would be glad to correct this in future editions.

INTRODUCTION

This anthology was a joy to edit. I hope many of its ingredients and flavours will arouse a gratifying frisson of recognition; with those voices perhaps less familiar to the reader providing a spicing of excitement. Good too if the selection further whets the appetite for the richly diverse traditions on which it draws, and encourages a search for more work by those poets represented.

From the outset it was intended that the volume would incorporate the shortlist of a bbc Radio Scotland survey to find 'the nation's favourite Scottish poem' – the remaining eighty or so places being left at my disposal. Topping this shortlist were 'Tam O Shanter' and 'A Man's a Man'. The sentiments of the latter struck me as ideal to open the book. And all but a few of the other poets would have been in a selection of my own, though not necessarily represented by the poem appearing here.

What took me aback was not any one oddity of inclusion, so much as the complete absence of the ballads: a treasure-trove of our culture, and (so I'd thought) enduringly 'popular'. Does their omission reflect a demographic eccentricity or age bias in the voting pattern, or suggest they are no longer taught in schools... or handed down, in childhood?

Either way, my instant response was to include several, from the well-known narrative of 'Sir Patrick Spens' and the icy brevity of 'The Twa Corbies', to a version of 'The Two Sisters' whose uncanny closing stanzas make the hairs on the nape of my neck rise. Beyond this and suffusing the bloodstream of the volume are ballad elements past and present, from the Borders to Shetland. These rub shoulders with poems in English and Scots; the latter's urban and rural dialects – distinctive in orthography, cadence and social perspective – mining a seam from the Central Belt through Fife, Buchan and the 'cauld east countra', as far as the Orkneys.

I sought, too, what I hoped would constitute other 'favourites', on the basis of their presence in earlier anthologies or their appeal among poetry readers I sounded. Complementing these are more recent poems for which I have a fondness. I like to think they enhance the volume – and that their freshness, verve, ways of seeing, and at times their humour, will be enticing.

By this stage the selection process was instinctual, as against consciously planned. Rather than anguish (as I'd anticipated) over whom or what to include, I found poems suggesting themselves, often to my astonishment and seemingly out of the blue. One would 'speak to' or reveal correspondences with another, urging that they appear consecutively, or strike sparks off each other on facing pages. Two with the same title even came tapping at the door.

Above all I responded to poems I found not just memorable but accessible: meaning not simple or simplistic, or failing to reward rereading, but with a directness that went hand-in-hand with their formal and imaginative virtues. In pursuit of this I may have ruffled a few feathers by favouring early work, on the grounds that this often displays a lucidity which subsequent complexity and 'maturity' can cloud. Nor beyond hinting (as with Dunbar) at strands and terrains, did I want a large number of poems needing glossed. Personal taste was a key factor: the final selection, to have character and an emotional identity, had to be filtered through my own feelings. In the choice of contemporaries, I hope I've caught something of today's spirit and multifarious music. As for sins of omission, any future anthology is as free to be of its own time and place.

This may relate particularly to Gaelic. Sorley MacLean's 'Hallaig', on the shortlist, is here in the original and in translation. I have not added others – because, not being a Gaelic speaker, I do not see that I could have done so competently. Who knows, this volume may be a spur to a Gaelic equivalent.

My thanks are due to Robyn Marsack to whom I put the idea for an anthology, and who as its enabling spirit proved the voice of reason and discretion; and to Gavin MacDougall and Catriona Vernal, of Luath Press, through whose commitment and care the project has borne fruit. A personal satisfaction is the publication of a Large Print version, along with the Luath edition. This stemmed from a conversation with a friend whose sight was rapidly deteriorating, and the confirmation of librarians I spoke to that there was room for such a volume. I am grateful to the rnib, and to Cleodie Mackinnon for sowing the seed.

Finally I thank those poets who provided biographical details and observations on their poems. I hope they will be pleased, if sometimes perhaps surprised, at the company they find themselves in.

STEWART CONN

1

A MAN'S A MAN FOR A' THAT

Robert Burns 1759–1796

Is there for honest poverty
   That hings his head, an' a' that?
The coward slave, we pass him by –
   We dare be poor for a' that!
For a' that, an a' that,
   Our toils obscure, an a' that,
The rank is but the guinea's stamp,
   The man's the gowd for a' that.

What tho' on hamely fare we dine,
   Wear hodden grey, an a' that?
Gie fools their silks, and knaves their wine –
   A man's a man for a' that!
For a' that, an' a' that,
   Their tinsel show, an' a' that,
The honest man, tho' e'er sae poor,
   Is king o' men for a' that.

Ye see yon birkie ca'd a lord,
   Wha struts, an' stares, an' a' that?
Tho' hundreds worship at his word,
   He's but a coof for a' that.
For a' that, an a' that,
   His ribband, star, an a' that,
The man o' independent mind,
   He looks an' laughs at a' that.

A prince can mak a belted knight,
  A marquis, duke, an a' that!
But an honest man's aboon his might –
  Gude faith, he mauna fa' that!
For a' that, an' a' that,
  Their dignities, an a' that,
The pith o' sense an' pride o' worth,
  Are higher rank than a' that.

Then let us pray that come it may
  As come it will for a' that –
That sense and worth o'er a' the earth,
  Shall bear the gree, an a' that.
For a' that, an a' that,
  It's comin yet for a' that,
That man to man the world o'er
  Shall brithers be for a' that.

2

LANDSCAPE WITH ONE FIGURE
Douglas Dunn b. 1942

Shipyard cranes have come down again
To drink at the river, turning their long necks
And saying to their reflections on the Clyde,
'How noble we are.'

Fields are waiting for them to come over.
Trees gesticulate into the rain,
The nerves of grasses quiver at their tips.
Come over and join us in the wet grass!

The wings of gulls in the distance wave
Like handkerchiefs after departing emigrants.
A tug sniffs up the river, looking like itself.
Waves fall from their small heights on river mud.

If I could sleep standing, I would wait here
For ever, become a landmark, something fixed
For tug crews or seabound passengers to point at,
An example of being a part of a place.

3

It was a day peculiar to this piece of the planet,
when larks rose on long thin strings of singing
and the air shifted with the shimmer of actual angels.
Greenness entered the body. The grasses
shivered with presences, and sunlight
stayed like a halo on hair and heather and hills.
Walking into town, I saw, in a radiant raincoat,
the woman from the fish-shop. 'What a day it is!'
cried I, like a sunstruck madman.
And what did she have to say for it?
Her brow grew bleak, her ancestors raged in their graves
as she spoke with their ancient misery:
'We'll pay for it, we'll pay for it, we'll pay for it!'

4

THE BONNIE EARL OF MORAY

Anon

Ye Highlands and ye Lawlands,
    Oh! where hae ye been?
They hae slain the Earl of Moray,
    And hae laid him on the green.

Now wae be to thee, Huntly,
    And wherefore did you sae?
I bade you bring him wi' you,
    But forbade you him to slay.

He was a braw gallant,
    And he rid at the ring;
And the bonnie Earl of Moray,
    Oh! he might hae been a king.

He was a braw gallant,
    And he play'd at the ba';
And the bonnie Earl of Moray
    Was the flower amang them a'.

He was a braw gallant,
    And he play'd at the glove;
And the bonnie Earl of Moray,
    Oh! he was the Queen's luve.

Oh! lang will his lady
   Look owre the castle Doune,
Ere she see the Earl of Moray
   Come sounding thro' the toun.

5

MEMORIAL OF ST COLUMBA

Anon, translated from Latin by Gilbert Márkus

Mouth of the dumb,
light of the blind,
foot of the lame,
to the fallen stretch out your hand.
Strengthen the senseless,
restore the mad.
O Columba, hope of Scots,
by your merits' mediation
make us companions
of the blessed angels.
          Alleluia.

6

John Purser b. 1942

I have tried to know suffering as the birds must know it
to hunger with the starved buzzard
to bruise as a battered redwing stupefied by storms
to share the cackling fears of the red heathercock.
I am no dove.

My pride has fed on corpses
stabbing the eye of knowledge
a raven pecking at meanings
wanting possession of dead things.

My pens were tugged from the wings of geese
hissing their innocence,
the skins of hollies stripped and boiled
and insects crushed for ink.
Over five hundred calves have crumpled to their knees
to yield pelts for my library of books.

Oh my God forgive! Forgive me — count my ribs —
I too have yielded one for Eves I never touched,
mine a princely negation
— through my coarse cloak they leave
their imprint on the strand —
I would have truly starved
but my kind acolyte slipped milk into my meal.

My only purity in song, I gladly sing.
My one sorrow in dying
to leave others sorrowing.

7

SCOTCH BROTH

Robert Crawford b. 1959

A soup so thick you could shake its hand
And stroll with it before dinner.

The face rising to its surface,
A rayfish waiting to be stroked,

Is the pustular, eat-me face of a crofter,
Turnipocephalic, white-haired.

Accepting all comers, it's still our nation's
Flagsoup, sip-soup; sip, sip, sip

At this other scotch made with mutton
That intoxicates only

With peas and potatoes, chewy uists of meat.
All races breathe over our bowl,

Inhaling Inverness and Rutherglen,
Waiting for a big, teuchtery face

To compose itself from carrots and barley
Rising up towards the spoon.

8

THE PUDDOCK

John M. Caie 1878–1949

A puddock sat by the lochan's brim,
An' he thocht there was never a puddock like him.
He sat on his hurdies, he waggled his legs,
An' cockit his heid as he glowered throu' the seggs.
The bigsy wee cratur' was feelin' that prood
He gapit his mou' an' he croakit oot lood:
'Gin ye'd a' like tae see a richt puddock,' quo' he,
'Yell never, I'll sweer, get a better nor me.
I've fem'lies an' wives an' a weel-plenished hame,
Wi' drink for my thrapple an' meat for my wame.
The lasses aye thocht me a fine strappin' chiel,
An' I ken I'm a rale bonny singer as weel.
I'm nae gaun tae blaw, but th' truth I maun tell –
I believe I'm the verra MacPuddock himsel'.'

A heron was hungry an' needin' tae sup,
Sae he nabbit th' puddock and gollup't him up;
Syne runkled his feathers: 'A peer thing,' quo' he,
'But – but puddocks is nae fat they eesed tae be.'

9

AT LINTON KIRK

Ron Butlin b. 1949

Linton Kirk is stone and timber hollowed out of air;
where stained glass darkening to shadow traces out
a present tense across the floor.

Our first weekend together: a night without much sleep,
a morning's levitation over hills and cold rain.
The visitor's book lies open. We flip the pages back
to catch sight of a world before we'd met,
then pause uncertain what to write. I glance outside:

an east wind scours the burnt yellow fields to black,
tearing colours from trees; the blunted edge of winter
    sunlight
hacks at names, dates and words of consolation;
the dead withdraw into the living.

Your scent, the blue-and-silver patterned scarf you wear,
our closeness – these are not memories.
Once we've signed the book and put the date we'll leave
and Linton Kirk stand empty.
How far into the future can I reach to take your hand?

10

ETTRICK

Lady John Scott 1810–1900

When we first rade down Ettrick,
Our bridles were ringing, our hearts were dancing,
The waters were singing, the sun was glancing,
An' blithely our voices rang out thegither,
As we brushed the dew frae the blooming heather,
　When we first rade down Ettrick.

When we next rade down Ettrick
The day was dying, the wild birds calling,
The wind was sighing, the leaves were falling,
An' silent an' weary, but closer thegither,
We urged our steeds thro' the faded heather,
　When we next rade down Ettrick.

When I last rade down Ettrick,
The winds were shifting, the storm was waking,
The snow was drifting, my heart was breaking,
For we never again were to ride thegither,
In sun or storm on the mountain heather,
　When I last rade down Ettrick.

11

BEACHCOMBER

George Mackay Brown 1921–1996

Monday I found a boot –
Rust and salt leather.
I gave it back to the sea, to dance in.

Tuesday a spar of timber worth thirty bob.
Next winter
It will be a chair, a coffin, a bed.

Wednesday a half can of Swedish spirits.
I tilted my head.
The shore was cold with mermaids and angels.

Thursday I got nothing, seaweed,
A whale bone,
Wet feet and a loud cough.

Friday I held a seaman's skull,
Sand spilling from it
The way time is told on kirkyard stones.

Saturday a barrel of sodden oranges.
A Spanish ship
Was wrecked last month at The Kame.

Sunday, for fear of the elders,
I sit on my bum.
What's heaven? A sea chest with a thousand gold coins.

12

O WALY, WALY

Anon

O waly, waly up the bank!
 And waly, waly, down the brae!
And waly, waly yon burn-side,
 Where I and my love wont to gae!

I lean'd my back unto an aik,
 I thought it was a trusty tree,
But first it bow'd, and syne it brak,
 Sae my true-love did lightly me.

O waly, waly! but love be bony
 A little time, while it is new,
But when 'tis auld, it waxeth cauld,
 And fades away like morning dew.

O wherefore should I busk my head?
 Or wherefore should I kame my hair?
For my true-love has me forsook,
 And says he'll never love me mair.

Now Arthur-Seat shall be my bed,
 The sheets shall ne'er be fyl'd by me
Saint Anton's well shall be my drink,
 Since my true-love has forsaken me.

Martinmas wind, when' wilt thou blaw,
    And shake the green leaves off the tree?
O gentle death, when wilt thou come?
    For of my life I am weary.

'Tis not the frost that freezes fell,
    Nor blawing snaw's inclemency;
'Tis not sic cauld that makes me cry,
    But my love's heart grown cauld to me.

When we came in by Glasgow town,
    We were a comely sight to see,
My love was cled in the black velvet,
    And I my sell in cramasie.

But had I wist, before I kiss'd,
    That love had been sae ill to win,
I'd lock'd my heart in a case of gold,
    And pin'd it with a silver pin.

Oh, oh, if my young babe were born,
    And set upon the nurse's knee,
And I my sell were dead and gane!
    For a maid again I'll never be.

13

Above Tweed Green levels
Maeve first raises the harp.

Prosper her hand that plucks
then clenches fist like a jockey.

Grip inside thighs
the colt with a cropped mane.

Turn blades on the curved neck
bristling with spigots.

Out from the rosewood forest
came this foal of strung nerve.

Stand in your grainy coat,
let her lift elbows over you.

Keep her thumbs bent
and fingers hard to do the playing.

Eight summers made them, clarsach,
I freely give you my elder daughter.

14

THE LAIRD O' COCKPEN

Carolina Oliphant, Lady Nairne 1766–1845

The Laird o' Cockpen, he's proud an' he's freat,
His mind is ta'en up wi' the things o' the state;
He wanted a wife his braw house to keep,
But favour wi' wooin' was fashious to seek.

Doun by the dyke-side a lady did dwell,
At his table-head he thought she'd look well;
M'Cleish's ae daughter o' Claverse-ha Lee,
A penniless lass wi' a lang pedigree.

His wig was well pouther'd, and as guid as new,
His waistcoat was white, his coat it was blue;
He put on a ring, a sword, and cock'd hat
And wha could refuse the laird wi' a' that?

He took the grey mare, and rade cannilie,
And rapp'd at the yett o' Claverse-ha Lee:
'Gae tell Mistress Jean to come speedily ben,
She's wanted to speak to the laird o' Cockpen.'

Mistress Jean was makin' the elder-flower wine:
'And what brings the laird at sic a like time?'
She put off her apron and on her silk gown,
Her mutch wi' red ribbons, and gaed awa' doun.

And when she cam' ben, he bowed fu' low,
And what was his errand he soon let her know;
Amazed was the laird when the lady said 'Na';
And wi' a laigh curtsie she turned awa'.

Dumfounder'd he was, nae sigh did he gie,
He mounted his mare and he rade cannilie;
And often he thought, as he gaed thro' the glen,
She's daft to refuse the laird o' Cockpen.

15

A WINTER MORNING

Gerry Cambridge b. 1959

At age 14, Ayrshire

Puddle ice cracked like lightbulb glass.
Frost had furred the last of the hips and haws.
My breath plumed out like a dragon's
In the cheering cold that morning the class
Was off for the day as the heating had failed –
Off for the week, with luck.

It was a gift, an escape from the wise laws
That governed things, a glimpse
Of possibility, like the thought
Of seeing a waxwing in an Irvine garden,
Or discovering a girl who liked you,
Or waking to find tremendous snow.
Not the escape itself, but its fine surprise.

16

AILSA CRAIG

Gerald Mangan b. 1951

It bulked large above my sandcastles:
a stepping-stone from a land of giants,
with a noose of surf around its neck.

One blustery sunset, turning purple,
it reared above my father's head
as he slammed outdoors from a row,

to sulk on the fuming causeway.
Geysers of spume were spouting high
as he strode down past the warning-signs,

and the last light was a hellish red
as he dwindled, stooping, into the rocks,
and drowned in my streaming eyes.

He'll be right back, my mother said.
But I saw the Irish Sea overwhelm
a rage that could shake a tenement.

He'd never looked so small, and wrong.
I never knew what drove him there,
but I saw him thrashed by a stormy God,

and he never seemed so tall again.
I'd never seen him so whole, before
I saw that tombstone over his head.

17

SIR PATRICK SPENS

Anon

The king sits in Dumfermline toun,
  Drinking the blood-reid wine:
'O whaur will I get skeely skipper,
  To sail this new ship of mine?'

An' up and spake an eldern knicht,
  Sat at the kings richt knee:
'Sir Patrick Spens is the best sailor
  That ever sail'd the sea.'

The king has written a braid letter,
  And sealed it wi' his hand,
And sent it to Sir Patrick Spens,
  Was walking on the strand.

'To Noroway, to Noroway
  To Noroway o'er the faem,
The king's dauchter of Noroway,
  'Tis thou maun bring her hame.'

The first line that Sir Patrick read,
  So loud, loud lauched he;
The neist line that Sir Patrick read.
  The tear blinded his ee.

'O wha is this has done this deid,
    This ill deid done to me,
To send me out this time o' the year,
    To sail upon the sea?

'Be it wind, be it weet, be it hail, be it sleet,
    Our ship maun sail the faem;
The king's daughter o' Noroway,
    'Tis we maun fetch her hame.'

They hoysed their sails on Monenday morn,
    Wi a' the speed they may;
They hae landed in Noroway,
    Upon a Wodensday.

They hadna been a week, a week
    In Noroway but twae,
When that the lords o' Noroway
    Began aloud to say:

'Ye Scottishmen spend a' our king's goud,
    And a' our queenis fee!'
'Ye lie, ye lie, ye liars loud,
    Sae loud I hear ye lie!

'For I hae brought as much o' the white money
    As gane my men and me,
And I brought a half fou o' gude red goud
    Oot o'er the sea wi' me.

'Mak ready, mak ready, my merry men a',
    Our gude ship sails the morn.'
'Now ever alack, my maister dear,
    For I fear a deadly storm.

'I saw the new mune late yestreen,
     Wi the auld mune in her arm,
And I fear, I fear, my maister dear,
     That we will come to harm.'

They hadna sailed a league, a league,
     A league but barely three,
When the lift grew dark, and the wind blew loud,
     And gurly grew the sea.

The ankers brak, and the tapmasts lap,
     It was sic a deidly storm,
And the waves came o'er the broken ship,
     Till a' her sides were torn.

'O whaur will I get a gude sailor,
     To tak the helm in hand,
Till I get up to the tall tapmast,
     To see if I can spy land?'

'O here am I, a sailor gude,
     To tak the helm in hand,
Till you go up to the tall tapmast;
     But I fear you'll ne'er spy land.'

He hadna gane a step, a step,
     A step but barely ane,
When a bout flew out of our goodly ship,
     And the saut sea it cam in.

'Gae fetch a web o' the silken claith,
     Anither o' the twine,
And wap them into our gude ship's side,
     And let na the sea come in.'

They fetched a web o' the silken claith,
    Anither o' the twine,
And they wapped them into that gude ship's side,
    But still the sea cam in.

O laith, laith were our gude Scots lords
    To weet their cork-heeled shoon;
But lang or a' the play was played,
    They wat their hats aboon.

And mony was the feather-bed
    That flottered on the faem,
And mony was the gude lord's son
    That never mair cam hame.

O lang, lang may the ladies sit,
    Wi their fans intil their hand,
Or eir they see Sir Patrick Spens
    Cum sailing to the land.

O lang, lang may the maidens sit,
    Wi their gowd kames in their hair,
Waiting for their ain deir lords,
    For them they'll see nay mair.

Half owre, half owre to Aberdour,
    'Tis fiftie fadom deip,
And thair lies guid Sir Patrick Spens,
    Wi the Scots lords at his feit.

18

LUSS VILLAGE

Iain Crichton Smith (Iain Mac A'Gobhainn) 1928–1998

Such walls, like honey, and the old are happy
in morphean air like gold-fish in a bowl.
Ripe roses trail their margins down a sleepy
mediaeval treatise on the slumbering soul.

And even the water, fabulously silent,
has no salt tales to tell us, nor makes jokes
about the yokel mountains, huge and patient,
that will not court her but read shadowy books.

A world so long departed! In the churchyard
the tilted tombs still gossip, and the leaves
of stony testaments are read by Richard,
Jean and Carol, pert among the sheaves

of unscythed shadows, while the noon day hums
with bees and water and the ghosts of psalms.

19

A SCENTED GARDEN
Tessa Ransford b. 1939

Peebles has a scented garden
'for the blind,' planted beside the river
opposite the modern swimming pool.

Unblind, I close my eyes to breathe
and listen: a linnet is singing
in lemon-scented leaves.

I imagine orange blossom with roses,
frangipani and hyacinth.
East and west are met in the scented garden.

Blindly I acquiesce. My east and west,
synthetic, abolish the dualities
that sight imposes on our world.

The river chants its plainsong.
I open my eyes. You are watching me, smiling.
I take your hand and lead you down the street.

20

GOLLOP'S

Anna Crowe b. 1945

Gollop was our grandmother's butcher.
Saying his name out loud, you swallowed
a lump of gristle whole. Even the thought
of going to Gollop's made us gulp,
made my little green-eyed sister's eyes
grow rounder, greener. Swags of rabbits
dangled at the door in furry curtains;
their eyes milky, blood congealed
around their mouths like blackcurrant-jelly.
You'd to run a gauntlet of paws.

Inside, that smell of blood and sawdust
still in my nostrils. Noises. The thump
as a cleaver fell; flinchings, aftershocks
as sinews parted, bone splintered.
The wet rasp of a saw. My eyes
were level with the chopping bench.
Its yellow wood dipped in the middle
like the bed I shared with Rosy.
Sometimes a trapdoor in the floor
was folded back. Through clouds of frost
our eyes made out wooden steps, then
huge shapes shawled in ice – the cold-store.

Into which the butcher fell,
once, bloody apron and all.
When my grandparents went to see
Don Juan, and told us how it ended
– *Like Mr Gollop!* I whispered.
Mr Gollop only broke his leg, but

>   *Crash! Bang! Wallop!*
>   *Went Mr Gollop!*

we chanted from our sagging bed,
giggles celebrating his downfall,
cancelling his nasty shop.
As the Co-op did a few years later
when it opened on the High Street.
Giving him the chop.

MARY'S SONG

Marion Angus 1854–1944

I wad ha'e gi'en him my lips tae kiss,
Had I been his, had I been his;
Barley breid and elder wine,
Had I been his as he is mine.

The wanderin' bee it seeks the rose;
Tae the lochan's bosom the burnie goes;
The grey bird cries at evenin's fa',
'My luve, my fair one, come awa'.'

My beloved sall ha'e this he'rt tae break,
Reid, reid wine and the barley cake;
A he'rt tae break, an' a mou' tae kiss,
Tho' he be nae mine, as I am his.

22

SARAH: FED UP

Janet Paisley b. 1948

See ma mammy,
says eat yer dinner.
Gies me cabbidge.
See ma granny,
says the wean
wullnae eat that,
leave it, hen.
Gies me choclit.
See ma daddy,
says ah've goatie
clear ma plate.
Dinnae like that
greasy gravy,
stane cauld tatties.
See ma granda,
says the bairn
s'no goat a stummick
like a coo.
Gies me lickris,
pandrops, chews.
Ett thum aw.
Feel seek noo.

23

MACPHERSON'S RANT

Anon

Fare ye weel ye dark and lonely hills,
Far away beneath the sky.
Macpherson's time will not he long
On yonder gallows tree.

    Sae rantinly, sae wantonly,
    Sae dantinly gaed he.
    He played a tune, an he danced it roon,
    Ablow the gallows tree.

It was by a woman's treacherous hand
That I was condemned tae dee.
Upon a ledge at a window she stood
And a blanket she threw ower me.

The Laird o' Grant, that Hieland saunt,
That first laid hands on me.
He pleads the cause o' Peter Broon,
Tae let Macpherson dee.

Untie these bands frae off my hands
An' gie tae me my sword,
An' there's no a man in a' Scotland
But I'll brave him at a word.

For there's some come here tae see me hanged
An' some tae buy my fiddle
But before that I do part wi' her
I'll brak her through the middle.

He took the fiddle intae baith o' his hands
An' he brak it ower a stane.
Says no anither hand shall play on thee
When I am deid an' gane.

Farewell my ain dear Highland hame,
Fareweel my wife an' bairns.
There was nae repentance in my hert
When my fiddle was in my airms.

O, little did my mither think
When first she cradled me
That I would turn a rovin' boy
An' die on a gallows tree.

The reprieve was comin' ower the Brig o' Banff
Tae set Macpherson free.
Bit they pit the clock a quarter afore
An' they hanged him tae the tree.

24

DID YE SEE ME?

Robert Garioch 1909–1981

I'll tell ye of ane great occasioun:
I tuke pairt in a graund receptioun.
Ye canna hae the least perceptioun
how pleased I was to get the invitatioun

tae assist at ane dedicatioun.
And richtlie sae; frae its inceptioun
the hale ploy was my ain conceptioun:
I was asked to gie a dissertatioun.

The function was held in the aipen air,
a peety, that; the keelies of the toun,
a toozie lot, gat word of the affair.

We cudnae stop it: they jist gaithert roun
to mak sarcastic cracks and grin and stare.
I wisht I hadnae worn my MA goun.

25

THE WILD GEESE

Violet Jacob 1863–1946

'Oh, tell me what was on yer road, ye roarin' norlan'
  wind
As ye cam' blawin' frae the land that's niver frae my
  mind?
My feet they trayvel England, but I'm deein' for the north –'
'My man, I heard the siller tides rin up the Firth o' Forth.'

'Aye, Wind, I ken them well eneuch, and fine they fa'
  and rise,
And fain I'd feel the creepin' mist on yonder shore that
  lies,
But tell me, ere ye passed them by, what saw ye on the
  way?'
'My man, I rocked the rovin' gulls that sail abune the Tay.'

'But saw ye naethin', leein' Wind, afore ye cam to Fife?
There's muckle lyin' yont the Tay that's mair to me nor life.'
'My man, I swept the Angus braes ye haena trod for years –'
'O wind, forgie a hameless loon that canna see for tears!'

'And far abune the Angus straths I saw the wild geese flee,
A lang, lang skein o' beatin' wings wi' their heids towards
  the sea,
And aye their cryin' voices trailed ahint them on the air –'
'O Wind, hae maircy, haud yer whisht, for I daurna listen
  mair!'

ON A CAT, AGEING

Alexander Gray 1882–1968

He blinks upon the hearth-rug,
   And yawns in deep content,
Accepting all the comforts
   That Providence has sent.

Louder he purrs and louder,
   In one glad hymn of praise
For all the night's adventures,
   For quiet and restful days.

Life will go on for ever,
   With all that cat can wish;
Warmth and the glad procession
   Of fish and milk and fish.

Only – the thought disturbs him –
   He's noticed once or twice,
The times are somehow breeding
   A nimbler race of mice.

27

THE COMING OF THE WEE MALKIES

Stephen Mulrine b. 1937

Whit'll ye dae when the wee Malkies come,
if they dreep doon affy the wash-hoose dyke,
an pit the hems oan the sterrheid light,
an play wee heidies oan the clean close-wa,
an bloo'er yir windae in wi the baw,
missis, whit'll ye dae?

Whit'll ye dae when the wee Malkies come,
if they chap yir door an choke yir drains,
an caw the feet fae yir sapsy weans,
an tummle thur wulkies through yir sheets,
an tim thur ashes oot in the street,
missis, whit'll ye dae?

Whit'll ye dae when the wee Malkies come,
if they chuck thur screwtaps doon the pan,
an stick the heid oan the sanit'ry man;
when ye hear thum shauchlin doon yir loaby,
chantin, 'Wee Malkies! The gemme's a bogey!'
Haw, missis, whit'll ye dae?

28

VIEW OF SCOTLAND / LOVE POEM

Liz Lochhead b. 1947

Down on her hands and knees
at ten at night on Hogmanay,
my mother still giving it elbowgrease
jiffywaxing the vinolay. (This is too
ordinary to be nostalgia.) On the kitchen table
a newly opened tin of sockeye salmon.
Though we do not expect anyone,
the slab of black bun,
petticoat-tails fanned out
on bone china.
'Last year it was very quiet...'

Mum's got her rollers in with waveset
and her well-pressed good dress
slack across the candlewick upstairs.
Nearly half-ten already and her not shifted!
If we're to even hope to prosper
this midnight must find us
how we would like to be.
A new view of Scotland
with a dangling calendar
is propped under last year's,
ready to take its place.

Darling, it's thirty years since
anybody was able to trick me,
December thirtyfirst, into
'looking into a mirror to see a lassie
wi' as minny heids as days in the year' –
and two already since,
familiar strangers at a party,
we did not know that we were
the happiness we wished each other
when the Bells went, did we?

All over the city
off-licences pull down their shutters,
people make for where they want to be
to bring the new year in.
In highrises and tenements
sunburst clocks tick
on dusted mantelshelves.
Everyone puts on their best spread of plenty
(for to even hope to prosper
this midnight must find us
how we would like to be).
So there's a bottle of sickly liqueur
among the booze in the alcove,
golden crusts on steak pies
like quilts on a double bed.
And this is where we live.
There is no time like the
present for a kiss.

29

Sir Walter Scott 1771–1832

Proud Maisie is in the wood,
    Walking so early.
Sweet Robin sits on the bush,
    Singing so rarely.

'Tell me, thou bonny bird,
    When shall I marry me?'
'When six braw gentlemen
    Kirkward shall carry ye.'

'Who makes the bridal bed,
    Birdie, say truly?'
'The grey-headed sexton,
    That delves the grave duly.

'The glowworm o'er grave and stone
    Shall light thee steady;
The owl from the steeple sing,
    'Welcome, proud lady.' '

THE STRANGER

Elizabeth Burns b. 1957

Waking in the half-light of a summer night
when the sky is milky grey
and the garden faded to pastels
   – pale roses, a creamy haze of elderflower –
I wander the quiet corridor
of this house where I'm a stranger

and passing by an open door,
I glimpse her in a mirror,
a figure in an old print nightgown
— belly round as the full moon
that floated low over the barn –
and see her for a moment as ghost,
as someone from another time, someone
who is not myself

for as the old house holds within its walls
something of all those who've ever lived here,
so this stranger's flesh and bone enfold
another soul

the unknown lodger in, my body
making ready for the daybreak
about to crack the darkness
and enter into light –

31

BABY IN THE DAFFODILS

Gillian K. Ferguson b. 1965

We plump you in a flock of daffodils,
a migration on stalks, a common motion,

earth's blonde spring hair ruffled
by affectionate wind. *Yes, yes, yes,*

they agree. *Yes, yes, yes,* madly
nodding. *We love your baby,*

he is more like us than you. New.
Our buds unfurl like fresh fingers

petals soft as skin; his blood is clear
as sap, he has our colouring,

yellow curls, sky in his eyes,
cheeks blowing. They bend

over you like anxious aunties,
all kissing at once. You grab

a hooked green throat,
stuff its open golden mouth

into your own tight rose.
With two teeth and cat's

tongue you eat a flower,
smiling like a young god

accustomed to nectar.
How they laugh hysterically

en masse, indulgently shining
in your face like sun.

32

It's fine when ye stand in a queue
at the door o' the 'Dole'
on a snawy day,
To ken that ye leive in the bonniest
land in the world,
The bravest, tae.

It's fine when you're in a pickle
Whether or no'
you'll get your 'dough,'
To sing a wee bit sang
o' the heather hills,
And the glens below.

It's fine when the clerk says,
'Nae "dole" here for you!'
To proodly turn,
and think o' the bluidy slashin'
the English got
at Bannockburn.

33

CUDDLE DOON

Alexander Anderson 1845–1909

The bairnies cuddle doon at nicht
    Wi' muckle faucht an' din –
'O, try and sleep, ye waukrife rogues,
    Your faither's comin' in' –
They never heed a word I speak;
    I try to gi'e a froon,
But aye I hap them up, an' cry,
    'O, bairnies, cuddle doon.'

Wee Jamie wi' the curly heid –
    He aye sleeps next the wa' –
Bangs up an' cries, 'I want a piece' –
    The rascal starts them a'.
I rin an' fetch them pieces, drinks,
    They stop awee the soun',
Then draw the blankets up an' cry,
    'Noo, weanies, cuddle doon.'

But ere five minutes gang, wee Rab
    Cries oot, frae 'neath the claes,
'Mither, mak' Tam gi'e ower at ance,
    He's kittling wi' his taes.'
The mischief's in that Tam for tricks,
    He'd bother half the toon;
But aye I hap them up, and cry,
    'O, bairnies, cuddle doon.'

At length they hear their faither's fit,
    An', as he steeks the door,
They turn their faces to the wa',
    While Tam pretends to snore.
'Ha'e a' the weans been gude?' he asks,
    As he pits aff his shoon.
'The bairnies, John, are in their beds,
    An' lang since cuddled doon.'

An' just afore we bed oorsel's,
    We look at oor wee lambs;
Tam has his airm roun' wee Rab's neck,
    An' Rab his airm roun' Tam's.
I lift wee Jamie up the bed,
    An', as I straik each croon,
I whisper, till my heart fills up,
    'O, bairnies, cuddle doon.'

The bairnies cuddle doon at nicht
    Wi' mirth that's dear to me;
But sune the big warl's cark an' care
    Will quaten doon their glee.
Yet, come what will to ilka ane,
    May He who rules aboon
Aye whisper, though their pows be bald,
    'O, bairnies, cuddle doon.'

34

FLOWERS OF THE FOREST

Jean Elliot 1727–1805

I've heard the lilting at our yowe-milking,
  Lasses a-lilting before the dawn o' day;
But now they are moaning on ilka green loaning:
  'The Flowers of the Forest are a' wede away.'

At buchts, in the morning, nae blythe lads are scorning:
  The lasses are lonely, and dowie, and wae:
Nae daffin', nae gabbin', but sighing and sabbing:
  Ilk ane lifts her leglen, and hies her away.

In hairst, at the shearing, nae youths now are jeering,
  The bandsters are lyart, and runkled and grey;
At fair or at preaching, nae wooing, nae fleeching:
  The Flowers of the Forest are a' wede away.

At een, in the gloaming, nae swankies are roaming
  'Bout stacks wi' the lasses at bogle to play,
But ilk ane sits drearie, lamenting her dearie:
  The Flowers of the Forest are a' wede away.

Dule and wae for the order sent out lads to the Border:
    The English, for ance, by guile wan the day:
The Flowers of the Forest, that foucht aye the foremost,
    The prime o' our land are cauld in the clay.

We'll hear nae mair lilting at the yowe-milking,
    Women and bairns are heartless and wae;
Sighing and moaning on ilka green loaning:
    'The Flowers of the Forest are a' wede away.'

lilting: singing; *loaning*: pasture; *buchts*: sheepfolds; *daffin'*: fooling
around; *leglen*: milkpail; *lyart*: grizzled; *fleeching: coaxing or flattering*

35

HOUSE WITH POPLAR TREES

James Aitchison b. 1938

At the far end of the towering poplar lines
his house soars. From the upper window
he oversaw his land, his farms, his mines.
He watched his poplars and his slagheaps grow.

The earth, the coal beneath the earth, the air
above, whatever breathed the air – yes, these
hirelings bonded at the yearly fair –
were his. Behind his screen of poplar trees

The place still stands today. The entrance hall
is deep in daisies, buttercups, rough grass;
the main doorway has fallen from its wall
in the crumbling remnant of the roofless house.

Nearby a dim-eyed unworked Clydesdale feeds
on what was once the lawn. You'd think a breeze
might bring the ruin down, or moss, or weeds,
behind the screen of towering poplar trees.

36

THE MAN WHO WANTED TO HUG COWS
Jim Carruth b. 1963

On his good days, he'd walk out from the village,
lose himself in country lanes, drawing blood from brambles
or stare across fields mumbling to himself.
They called him professor though no one knew his past;
the postman brought rumours of separation and break-
  down.

When first asked, farmers said no.
One relented, pointing him to a quiet Friesian.
'Seemed harmless enough' he told his neighbour later
but he watched him closely from the gate that first time,
uneasy at the nervousness of the stranger.

Left in peace, for long afternoons
he'd cling around folds of the heifer's neck;
whisper an echo in the beast's dark ear,
her big eyes and soft rough muzzle would turn to him.
Slow-motion slavers and heavy breath fell across his face.

To those who listen the farmer's wife still recalls
finding him asleep in the grass – a smile within the herd;
his head resting on thick-haired warmth,
lulled by the rise and fall of maternal ribs,
the beat of a larger heart.

37

from AULD REIKIE

Robert Fergusson 1750–1774

Auld Reikie! wale o' ilka town
That Scotland kens beneath the moon:
Whare couthy chields at e'ening meet
Their bizzin craigs and mou's to weet;
And blithely gar auld Care gae by
Wi' blinkin and wi' bleerin eye...

Now Morn, with bonny purple smiles,
Kisses the air-cock o' Saunt Giles;
Rakin their een, the servant lasses
Early begin their lies and clashes.
Ilk tells her friend of saddest distress,
That still she bruiks frae scoulin' mistress,
And wi' her joe in turnpike stair,
She'd rather snuff the stinkin air
As be subjected to her tongue,
Whan justly censur'd i' the wrong...

On stair, wi' tub or pat in hand,
The barefoot housemaids loe to stand,
That antrin fock may ken how snell
Auld Reikie will at mornin smell:
Then, with an inundation big as
The burn that 'neath the Nor' Brig is,
They kindly shower Edina's roses,
To quicken and regale our noses.

38

SEAGULL

Brian McCabe b. 1951

We are the dawn marauders.
We prey on pizza. We kill kebabs.
We mug thrushes for bread crusts
with a snap of our big bent beaks.
We drum the worms from the ground
with the stamp of our wide webbed feet.
We spread out, cover the area –
like cops looking for the body
of a murdered fish-supper.
Here we go with our hooligan yells
loud with gluttony, sharp with starvation.
Here we go bungee-jumping on the wind,
charging from the cold sea of our birth.
This is invasion. This is occupation.
Our flags are black, white and grey.
Our wing-stripes are our rank.
No sun can match the brazen
colour of our mad yellow eyes.

We are the seagulls.
We are the people.

39

Charles Murray 1864–1941

Gin I was God, sittin' up there abeen,
Weariet nae doot noo a' my darg was deen,
Deaved wi' the harps an' hymns oonendin' ringin',
Tired o' the flockin' angels hairse wi' singin',
To some clood-edge I'd daunder furth an', feth,
Look owre an' watch hoo things were gyaun aneth.
Syne, gin I saw hoo men I'd made mysel'
Had startit in to pooshan, sheet an' fell,
To reive an' rape, an' fairly mak' a hell
O' my braw birlin' Earth, – a hale week's wark –
I'd cast my coat again, rowe up my sark,
An', or they'd time to lench a second ark,
Tak' back my word an' sen' anither spate,
Droon oot the hale hypothec, dicht the sklate,
Own my mistak', an', aince I'd cleared the brod,
Start a'thing ower again, gin I was God.

40

Charles, Lord Neaves 1800–1876

We zealots, made up of stiff clay,
    The sour-looking children of sorrow,
While not over-jolly today,
    Resolve to be wretched tomorrow.
We can't for a certainty tell
    What mirth may molest us on Monday;
But, at least, to begin the week well,
    Let us all be unhappy on Sunday.

That day, the calm season of rest,
    Shall come to us freezing and frigid;
A gloom all our thoughts shall invest,
    Such as Calvin would call over-rigid,
With sermons from morning to night,
    We'll strive to be decent and dreary:
To preachers a praise and delight,
    Who ne'er think that sermons can weary…

What though a good precept we strain
    Till hateful and hurtful we make it!
What though, in thus pulling the rein,
    We may draw it as tight as to break it!
Abroad we forbid folks to roam,
    For fear they get social or frisky;
But of course they can sit still at home,
    And get dismally drunk upon whisky.

Then, though we can't certainly tell
    How mirth may molest us on Monday;
At least, to begin the week well,
    Let us all be unhappy on Sunday.

41

THE VOYEUR

Tom Leonard b. 1944

what's your favourite word dearie
is it wee
I hope it's wee
wee's such a nice wee word
like a wee hairy dog
with two wee eyes
such a nice wee word to play with dearie
you can say it quickly
with a wee smile
and a wee glance to the side
or you can say it slowly dearie
with your mouth a wee bit open
and a wee sigh dearie
a wee sigh
put your wee head on my shoulder dearie
oh my
a great wee word
and Scottish
it makes you proud

42

TO ALEXANDER GRAHAM

W.S. Graham 1918–1986

Lying asleep walking
Last night I met my father
Who seemed pleased to see me.
He wanted to speak. I saw
His mouth saying something
But the dream had no sound.

We were surrounded by
Laid-up paddle steamers
In The Old Quay in Greenock.
I smelt the tar and the ropes.

It seemed that I was standing
Beside the big iron cannon
The tugs used to tie up to
When I was a boy. I turned
To see Dad standing just
Across the causeway under
That one lamp they keep on.

He recognised me immediately.
I could see that. He was
The handsome, same age
With his good brows as when
He would take me on Sundays
Saying we'll go for a walk.

Dad, what am I doing here?
What is it I am doing now?
Are you proud of me?
Going away, I knew
You wanted to tell me something.

You stopped and almost turned back
To say something. My father,
I try to be the best
In you you give me always.

Lying asleep turning
Round in the quay-lit dark
It was my father standing
As real as life. I smelt
The quay's tar and the ropes.

I think he wanted to speak.
But the dream had no sound.
I think I must have loved him.

THE DELUGE

W.D. Cocker 1882–1970

The Lord took a staw at mankind,
A righteous an' natural scunner;
They were neither to haud nor to bind,
They were frichtit nae mair wi' his thun'er.

They had broken ilk edic' an' law,
They had pitten his saints to the sword,
They had worshipped fause idols o' stane;
'I will thole it nae mair,' saith the Lord.

'I am weary wi' flytin' at folk;
I will dicht them clean oot frae my sicht;
But Noah, douce man, I will spare,
For he ettles, puir chiel, to dae richt.'

So he cried unto Noah ae day,
When naebody else was aboot,
Sayin': 'Harken, my servant, to Me
An' these, my commands, cairry oot:

'A great, muckle boat ye maun build,
An ark that can float heich an' dry,
Wi' room in't for a' yer ain folk
An' a hantle o' cattle forby.

'Then tak' ye the fowls o' the air,
Even unto big bubbly-jocks;
An' tak' ye the beasts o' the field:
Whittrocks, an' foumarts, an' brocks.

'Wale ye twa guid anes o' each,
See that nae cratur rebels;
Dinna ye fash aboot fish:
They can look efter theirsels.

'Herd them a' safely aboard,
An' ance the Blue Peter's unfurled,
I'll send doun a forty-day flood,
And de'il tak' the rest o' the world.'

Sae Noah wrocht hard at the job,
An' searched to the earth's farthest borders,
An' gethered the beasts an' the birds
An' tell't them to staun' by for orders.

An' his sons, Ham an' Japheth an' Shem,
Were thrang a' this time at the wark;
They had fell'd a wheen trees in the wood
An' biggit a great, muckle ark.

This wasna dune juist on the quate,
An' neebours would whiles gether roun';
Then Noah would drap them a hint
Like: 'The weather is gaun to break doun.'

But the neebours wi' evil were blin'
An' little jaloused what was wrang,
Sayin': 'That'll be guid for the neeps,'
Or: 'The weather's been drouthy ower lang.'

Then Noah wi' a' his ain folk,
An' the beasts an' the birds got aboard;
An' they steekit the door o' the ark,
An' they lippened theirsels to the Lord.

Then doun cam' a lashin' o' rain,
Like the wattest wat day in Lochaber;
The hailstanes like plunkers cam' stot,
An' the fields turned to glaur, an' syne glabber.

An' the burns a' cam' doun in a spate,
An' the rivers ran clean ower the haughs,
An' the brigs were a' soopit awa',
An' what had been dubs becam' lochs.

Then the folk were sair pitten aboot,
An' they cried, as the weather got waur:
'Oh! Lord, we ken fine we hae sinn'd,
But a joke can be cairried ower faur!'

Then they chapp'd at the ark's muckle door,
To speir gin douce Noah had room;
But Noah ne'er heedit their cries,
He said: 'This'll learn ye to soom.'

An' the river roar'd loudly an' deep;
An' the miller was droon't in the mill;
An' the watter spread ower a' the land,
An' the shepherd was droon't on the hill.

But Noah an' a' his ain folk,
Kep' safe frae the fate o' ill men,
Till the ark, when the flood had gi'en ower,
Cam' dunt on the tap o' a ben.

An' the watters row'd back to the seas,
An' the seas settled doun an' were calm.
An' Noah replenished the earth –
But they're sayin' he took a guid dram!

44

COUNTING SHEEP

Hamish Brown b. 1934

Sleep is postponed
when words sheep over
the gates of the mind.
It is too late, past dawn,
to gather wool from thorns
and barbed-wire fences.
The beasts have to be grabbed,
dipped and disinfected,
sheared in an hour
while fighting awake
hung-over from day.
Who would be a shepherd
with flocks of words loose
on the fells of the mind
in March moonlight?
I would wash my mind
of the stinking fold,
but I cannot sleep
till I count my sheep.

45

THE SHEPHERD'S HUT

Andrew Young 1885–1971

The smear of blue peat smoke
That staggered on the wind and broke,
The only sign of life,
Where was the shepherd's wife,
Who left those flapping clothes to dry,
Taking no thought for her family?
For, as they bellied out
And limbs took shape and waved about,
I thought, She little knows
That ghosts are trying on her children's clothes.

46

A MANIFESTO FOR MSPS

James Robertson b. 1958

Dinna be glaikit, dinna be ower smert,
dinna craw croose, dinna be unco blate,
dinna breenge in, dinna be ayewis late,
dinna steek yer lugs, dinna steek yer hert.
Dinna be sleekit, dinna be a sook,
dinna creesh nae loof for future favour,
dinna swick nor swither, hash nor haiver,
dinna be soor o face, and dinna jouk.
Open yer airms and minds tae folk in need,
hain frae fylin and skaith the land and sea,
tak tent o justice and the commonweal,
ding doon hypocrisy, wanthrift and greed,
heeze up the banner o humanity,
seek oot the truth and tae the truth be leal.

47

HATS

Muriel Spark 1918–2006

I was writing a poem called
    Hats.

I had seen a shop window
    in Venice, full of
        Hats.

There were hats for morning,
    for evening, men's hats, girls'
        Hats.

There were hats for fishing
And hats dating back to
    Death in Venice
His hat so Panama, hers such a
    Madame de Staël
        Hat.

I was writing a poem about
    Hats
Hats for a garden party, hats
For a wet day, hats for a
    wedding party, a
    memorial service.

There were hats for golf and
Hats for tennis. Bowler hats,
Top hats for the races, floral
    headgears equally.

And as I wrote this poem
Sitting in a square with my coffee,
I was called over to see a friend.
Only for an instant. I shoved
The poem in my handbag and
I slung the bag over the chair.

Only an instant.
And gone, gone forever, handbag
    poem, my hats, my hats.

Also my passport.
What was in the bag? said
    the policeman.

Some money, a passport
    and a poem.

How did it go, that poem?

        I wish I could remember.

48

HATS

Angela McSeveney b. 1964

My hats are stored in a column of boxes
bedded down like tortoises
in nests of tissue paper.

Some mornings I can dither
for half an hour before finally
settling on wearing perhaps

the mock suede turquoise toque
with a silver buckle or the big black felt one
plumed with an orange feather.

Till recently I'd no idea what
all this meant but now I know
my accessories are trimmed with intent.

Millinery hasn't been the same really
since reading in a footnote somewhere
that hats represent the genitalia, in Freud's opinion.

I've missed a lot of signals clearly
from closet obsessives, accosting me with compliments
or sometimes derision

like that respectable (or so I thought)
retired lady who leaned across the bus aisle
to admire the well worn, high crowned grey

(black ribbon, slanted brim)
that I had on that day.
When she was young, she said,

no-one left the house without a hat;
nice to see someone keeping the tradition up.
(Now what exactly was all that about?)

And I've been wrong to feel overlooked
and a little nettled even
that workmen never wolf-whistle

but now and then call down from on high
'I like the hat!' (I mean, what's wrong
with my chest, you big gorilla?)

And *in vino veritas* truly
as I suddenly remember
with a jolt of comprehension

the reeling drunk I neatly side stepped
as he leered towards me
at a bus stop in Leith, bellowing
'Nae offence like, lady,
but that's some fuckin' hat
– Ah jist hud tae tell ye'.

THE LAND O' CAKES
W.N. Herbert b. 1961

For Alee Esplin

Perched in their multi-storey flat
like a well-fed eagle, the skin
around my small aunt's eyes splintered
with staring into needless distances.

As if her countryside was made of cakes
she swept up great trays for us,
while my uncle disgorged awful jokes
with Eric Morecambe-like insouciance.

A glass cabinet held miniature beers,
dustless undrunk Guinnesses, light ales.
Once someone jumped from an upper floor
like jam on her spotless tablecloth.

She had diabetes suddenly; leaving
a ripped-off toe she plummeted too
in the hospital bed, grabbing onto us
like washing on the flashing balconies,

but she fell through pain like Alice
to me, and I thought she was constantly
halving her distance toward death
and would never smash, or like

an eagle losing its nerve, would pull
out of that dive. These days my uncle
stares at the distant bottles, stirs
his tea with a sugarless spoon.

50

AT THE PEATS

Alasdair Maclean 1926–1994

In March we start our harvesting.
We dig ourselves down out of sight
in a peat bog,
continuing perhaps all summer
when the weather lets us,
till the job is done.
My father and myself.
We work in harmony at first,
he cutting and I spreading,
backwards and forwards,
up and down,
the rhythm of the cradle.
Then in May the sun comes north,
thawing out the silence,
and the tourists sprout.
They prod us with their cameras,
making us aware of what we do,
and once we appeared in the *Scottish Field*
in a photograph so clear
you could count the midges.
Highland peasants cutting peat.
The abundance of free fuel
is an important factor in the crofting economy.
One of my father's rare grim smiles,
like a lull in the east wind,
broke out when I read that to him.

51

AUNT JULIA

Norman MacCaig 1910–1996

Aunt Julia spoke Gaelic
very loud and very fast.
I could not answer her –
I could not understand her.

She wore men's boots
when she wore any.
– I can see her strong foot,
stained with peat,
paddling with the treadle of the spinning-wheel
while her right hand drew yarn
marvellously out of the air.

Hers was the only house
where I've lain at night
in the absolute darkness
of a box bed, listening to
crickets being friendly.

She was buckets
and water flouncing into them.
She was winds pouring wetly
round house-ends.
She was brown eggs, black skirts
and a keeper of threepennybits
in a teapot.

Aunt Julia spoke Gaelic
very loud and very fast.
By the time I had learned
a little, she lay
silenced in the absolute black
of a sandy grave
at Luskentyre.
But I hear her still, welcoming me
with a seagull's voice
across a hundred yards
of peatscrapes and lazybeds
and getting angry, getting angry
with so many questions
unanswered.

GLASGOW SABBATH
Tom Buchan 1931–1995

Rum submerges
rain sheets off the dull heft of the Cuillin
ragged cattle
stand in their dunged pool at Elgol

and south by wet Mull
papercups half-buried in the beach at Dervaig
and the stunned Co-op van
with its turquoise sans serif motif

to the bubonic snatch of Glasgow
where volatile as monkeys
we die before our time
dazed with morphine in tiled wards

cloudcover sagging
a few stores open selling stale sliced bread
and coarse-faced couples
making for the coast

the streets littered
with hectic old women en route to vote for Christ
two or three late
croupiers and musicians in gabardine

and a high-stepping paranoiac
agitating his metabolism in the dank park
where laurels drip and pale red
goldfish ruffle the milky mucus on their skins.

53

THE TRYST

William Soutar 1898–1943

O luely, luely cam she in
And luely she lay doun:
I kent her be her caller lips
And her breists sae sma' and roun'.

A' thru the nicht we spak nae word
Nor sinder'd bane frae bane:
A' thru the nicht I heard her hert
Gang soundin' wi' my ain.

It was about the waukrife hour
When cocks begin to craw
That she smool'd saftly thru the mirk
Afore the day wud daw.

Sae luely, luely, cam she in
Sae luely was she gaen
And wi' her a' my simmer days
Like they had never been.

54

CANEDOLIA: AN OFF-CONCRETE SCOTCH FANTASIA

Edwin Morgan b. 1920

oa! hoy! awe! ba! mey!

who saw?
rhu saw rum. garve saw smoo. nigg saw tain. lairg saw
   lagg.
rigg saw eigg. largs saw haggs. tongue saw luss. mull
   saw yell.
stoer saw strone. drem saw muck. gask saw noss. unst
   saw cults.
echt saw banff. weem saw wick. trool saw twatt.

how far?
from largo to lunga from joppa to skibo from ratho to
   shona from
ulva to minto from tinto to tolsta from soutra to marsco
   from
braco to barra from alva to stobo from fogo to fada from
   gigha to
gogo from kelso to stroma from hirta to spango.

what is it like there?
och it's freuchie, it's faifley, it's wamphray, it's frandy, it's
   sliddery.

what do you do?
we foindle and fungle, we bonkle and meigle and max-
  poffle. we
scotstarvit, armit, wormit, and even whifflet. we play at
  crossstobs,
leuchars, gorbals and finfan. we scavaig, and there's aye
  a bit of
tilquhilly. if it's wet, treshnish and mishnish.

what is the best of the country?
blinkbonny! airgold! thundergay!

and the worst?
scrishven, shiskine, scrabster, and snizort.

listen! what's that?
catacol and wauchope, never heed them.

tell us about last night
well, we had a wee ferintosh and we lay on the quiraing.
  it was
pure strontian!

but who was there?
petermoidart and craigenkenneth and cambusputtock
  and
ecclemuchty and corriehulish and balladolly and
  altnacanny and
clauchanvrechan and stronachlochan and auchenlachar
  and
tighnacrankie and tilliebruaich and killieharra and
  invervannach
and achnatudlem and machrishellach and inchtamurchan
  and

auchterfechan and kinlochculter and ardnawhallie and
  invershuggle.

and what was the toast?
schiehallion! schiehallion! schiehallion!

THE CHARTRES OF GOWRIE

Don Paterson b. 1963

For T.H.

Late August, say the records, when the gowk-storm
shook itself out from a wisp of cloud
and sent them flying, their coats over their heads.
When every back was turned, the thunder-egg
thumped down in an empty barley-field.

No witness, then, and so we must imagine
everything, from the tiny crystal-stack,
its tingling light-code, the clear ripple of tines,
the shell snapping awake, the black rock
blooming through its heart like boiling tar,

to the great organ at dawn thundering away
half-a-mile up in the roof, still driving
each stone limb to its own extremity
and still unmanned, though if we find this hard
we may posit the autistic elder brother

of Maurice Duruflé or Messiaen.
Whatever, the reality is this:
at Errol, Grange, Longforgan, and St Madoes
they stand dumb in their doorframes, all agog
at the black ship moored in the sea of corn.

56

A JOY TA BEHOLD

Christine De Luca b. 1947

c. 1920
For my cousin, Douglas Smith

A young ting o lass gied ta guttin in Lerrick,
her arles lang paid an da money laid by.
Shö wis trang wi a laad wha hed little tae offer
bit a haert at wis honest an a smile at wis shy.

> *Haand owre haand we wir haulin an hailin*
> *affa Mousa, a catch a joy ta behold.*
> *Da dimriv wis spreadin, wir backs dey wir brakkin*
> *whin up i da net cam a brotch med o gowld.*

He'd gien tae da sea an saved aa his penga
an bowt her a brotch med o amber an gowld.
Shö voo'd shö wid wear hit tae aa but da guttin
ivery day o her life til gyaain twafaald.

Ee nicht shö sat mendin da nets fae da drifters,
da preen cam undön, da brotch fell on her lap.
Unawaar o her loss i da glim o da colly
shö rowed hit awa i da haert o da net.

Shö wis greetin an gowlin whinivver shö tocht on
da laad at hed gien her da boannie gowld brotch.
Wid he tink her dat haandless fur lossin da mindin
he'd browt fae da sailin ta seal der lovematch?

But he loved her far mair as her boannie blue een
an her hair at shone amber as fine as could be.
Da brotch hit could geng tae da depths o da ocean,
fur his love wis as wide as da airms o da sea.

A fisherman waeled hit oot fae da herrin:
hit kinda gied owre him; he medna a soond
but browt hit back hame tae his boannie young dowter
gyaain tae da guttin whin neist saison cam roond.

Dat young ting o lass gied ta guttin in Lerrick,
her arles lang paid an da money laid by.
Shö wis trang wi a laad wha hed little tae offer
bit a hert at wis honest an a smile at wis shy.

> *Haand owre haand we wir haulin an hailin*
> *affa Mousa, a catch a joy ta behold.*
> *Da dimriv wis spreadin, wir backs dey wir brakkin*
> *whin up i da net cam a brotch med o gowld.*

ting: little one; *arles*: down-payment to secure seasonal worker;
trang: courting; *hailin*: pulling fishing lines; *dimriv*: dawn; *gien tae
da sea*: joined Merchant Navy; *penga*: money; *gyaain*: going;
twafaald: doubled up, cripple; *preen*: pin; *colly*: small lamp; *mindin*: gift;
waeled: sifted, selected; *gied owre him*: unsettled him

57

APPLICATION

Diana Hendry b. 1941

O let me be your bidie-in
And keep you close within
As dearest kith and kin
I promise I'd be tidy in
Whatever bed or bunk you're in
I'd never ever drink your gin
I'd be your multi-vitamin
I'd wear my sexy tiger-skin
And play my love-sick mandolin
It cannot be a mortal sin
To be in such a dizzy spin
I'd like to get inside your skin
I'd even be your concubine
I hope you know I'm genuine
O let me be your bidie-in.

58

APPOINTMENT

Hamish Whyte b. 1947

Of course, you may be my bidie-in,
You didn't need to apply within.
A braw new world's about to begin,
We'll gang thegether through thick and thin,
We'll walk unscathed through burr and whin.
If you're to be my porcupin
I'll just have to bear it and grin.
I'll be your sheik, your djinn,
I'll be yang to your yin.
You'll be my kitten, my mitten, my terrapin.
All night long we'll make love's sweet din
And never mind the wheelie-bin.
In our romantic cin-
ema there'll be no FIN.
And so I say again – you're in –
You've got the job as bidie-in.

59

THE TWA CORBIES

Anon

As I was walking all alane,
I heard twa corbies making a mane;
The tane unto the t'other say,
'Where sall we gang and dine to-day?'

'In behint yon auld fail dyke,
I wot there lies a new-slain knight;
And naebody kens that he lies there,
But his hawk, his hound, and his lady fair.

'His hound is to the hunting gane,
His hawk, to fetch the wild-fowl hame,
His lady's ta'en another mate,
So we may mak our dinner sweet.

'Ye'll sit on his white hause-bane,
And I'll pike out his bonny blue een.
Wi' ae lock o' his gowden hair,
We'll theek our nest when it grows bare.

'Mony a ane for him makes mane,
But nane sall ken whare he is gane:
O'er his white banes, when they are bare,
The wind sall blaw for evermair.'

corbies: ravens; *mane*: moan; *the tane*: the one (as opposed to the other); *fail dyke*: turf wall; *hause-bane*: neck bone; *pike*: pick; *gowden*: golden; *theek*: thatch.

60

A SMALL WHITE DOG

Andrew Greig b. 1951

And when we die, they say,
a small white dog
trots into the big dark wood,
to do his business.

Or a woman steps from her dress,
walks along the broken jetty
to the end then dives
through light to liquid light.

I'm waiting on the bank
to see where she will reappear,
listening to a muffled bark
from the heart of the wood.

61

A NIGHT IN STOER LIGHTHOUSE

Ian McDonough b. 1955

Here a hungry man
could chew up the Atlantic
and still feel need of salt.

Can you smell the sun go down?
Extend a surreptitious hand to touch
the moon's deep cavities? A fox
surrounds the lighthouse with its bark.

Your body sprouts tattoos
of whaling ships: the eiderdown is sea-haar,
bedposts timbers decked in weeds.

I reach under green sheets to dredge
a bucketful of sailors, drowned
as drowned can be. A prowling moth
flaps round the lightbulb
in a breeze, traversing
all the open oceans of our dreams.

Blood atmospheres return, the walls
recalled by seagull tides of dawn. The fox
is earthed: the sun erects its peepshow
in a fragrant void.

62

THE OLD FISHERMAN
George Campbell Hay 1915–1984

Greet the bights that gave me shelter,
they will hide me no more with the horns of their
    forelands.
I peer in a haze, my back is stooping;
my dancing days for fishing are over.

The shoot that was straight in the wood withers,
the bracken shrinks red in the rain and shrivels,
the eyes that would gaze in the sun waver;
my dancing days for fishing are over.

The old boat must seek the shingle,
her wasting side hollow the gravel,
the hand that shakes must leave the tiller;
my dancing days for fishing are over.

The sea was good night and morning,
the winds were friends, the calm was kindly –
the snow seeks the burn, the brown fronds scatter;
my dancing days for fishing are over.

63

CHILDHOOD

Edwin Muir 1887–1959

Long time he lay upon the sunny hill,
　　To his father's house below securely bound.
Far off the silent, changing sound was still,
　　With the black islands lying thick around.

He saw each separate height, each vaguer hue,
　　Where the massed islands rolled in mist away,
And though all ran together in his view
　　He knew that unseen straits between them lay.

Often he wondered what new shores were there.
　　In thought he saw the still light on the sand,
The shallow water clear in tranquil air,
　　And walked through it in joy from strand to strand.

Over the sound a ship so slow would pass
　　That in the black hill's gloom it seemed to lie.
The evening sound was smooth like sunken glass,
　　And time seemed finished ere the ship passed by.

Grey tiny rocks slept round him where he lay,
　　Moveless as they, more still as evening came,
The grasses threw straight shadows far away,
　　　And from the house his mother called his name.

64

CRAGSMAN'S WIDOW

Robert Rendall 1898–1967

'He was aye vaigan b' the shore,
   An' climman amang the craigs,
 Swappan the mallimaks,
    Or taakan whitemaa aiggs.

'It's six year bye come Lammas,
   Sin' he gaed afore the face,
An' nane but an aald dune wife
    Was left tae work the place.

'Yet the sun shines doun on a' thing,
   The links are bonnie and green,
An' the sea keeps ebban an' flowan
    As though it had never been.'

mallimaks: fulmars.

65

SONG

Alan Spence b. 1947

the littlest bird
sang all for me
its song was love
it set me free

sang at my birth
and at my death
it sang its song
with my last breath

the littlest bird
sang in my soul
its song was joy
it made me whole

it made me whole
it set me free
it sang its song
its song was me

66

Anon

All wemen are guid, nobil and excellent
Wha can say that they ever do offend?
Daily they serve their God with gude intent
Sendil displease their husbands to life's end
Always but them to please they do intend.
Never man may find in them bruckilness
Sic qualities they still use, mair and less.

Reid this verse according to ye meitter
& it is guid of wemen but reid it to ye
nott* evin the contrair

*The subtly hidden alternative sense is revealed, by
inserting breath breaks at each X :*

All wemen are gude, nobil and excellent
Wha can say that   X   they ever do offend
Daily   X   they serve their God with gude intent
Sendil   X   displease their husbands to life's end
Always   X   but them to please they do intend.
Never   X   man may find in them bruckilness.   X
Sic qualities they still use, mair and less.

sendil: seldom; *bruckilness*: brittleness

67

Jim C. Wilson b. 1948

(Pompidou Centre, Paris)

Join me, quick, in my blue and yellow room
where the table and chair have wiggly legs
and the carpet has been autographed. Join
me for lunch: there's watermelon (mostly)
but, if you wish, four lemons as well. There's
strong yellow coffee to wash it all down
or, if you prefer, a cool greenish drink.
Later, the oil lamp can be lit. We'll watch
the sky, as squiggles of black slip away.
We'll slump by the blue rectangle, marvel
at six lemon leaves – so brilliantly,
unexpectedly green. You'll love my room;
you'll want to meet the designer. I call
him, simply, Henri: man of few colours,
fewer words. But an artist I believe.

68

THE EYE OF THE BEHOLDER

James McGonigal b. 1947

The garden pool's eye glazes
in a dream of evaporation: help I'm expiring
fern stems and sun's lips sucking
my water-skin tighter

quick fill me with tears – bucketfuls
of the shocking drops between lashes of bulrush.
Everything clouds, clears; three goldfish
gleam in a pupil appraising the blue

and in their midst, with dripping basin, you.

69

TO A LADYE

William Dunbar c.1460 – c.1520

Sweit rois of vertew and of gentilnes,
Delytsum lyllie of everie lustynes,
   Richest in bontie and in bewtie cleir,
   And everie vertew that is held most deir,
Except onlie that ye ar mercyless.

In to your garthe this day I did persew,
Thair saw I flowris that fresche wer of hew;
   Baithe quhyte and reid moist lusty wer to seyne,
   And halsum herbis upone stalkis grene;
Yit leif nor flour fynd could I nane of rew.

I dout that Merche, with his cauld blastis keyne,
Hes slane this gentill herbe, that I of mene,
   Quhois petewous deithe dois to my hart sic pane
   That I wald mak to plant his rute agane,
So confortand his levis unto me bene.

rois: rose; *lustynes*: loveliness; *bontie:* goodness; *garthe*: garden; *persew*: enter; *quhyte*: white; *halsum*: health-giving; *Yit leif nor flour fynd could I nane of rew*: Yet I could not find a leaf or flower of rue; *Merche*: March; *keyne*: fierce; *that I of mene*: of which I speak; *Quhois*: whose; *petewous*: piteous; *rute*: root; *confortand*: encouraging; *bene*: are.

70

from TO HIS MISTRESS

James Graham, Marquis of Montrose 1612–1650

My dear and only Love, I pray
   This noble World of thee,
Be govern'd by no other Sway
   But purest Monarchie.
For if Confusion have a Part,
   Which vertuous Souls abhore,
And hold a Synod in thy Heart,
   I'll never love thee more.

Like *Alexander* I will reign,
   And I will reign alone,
My Thoughts shall evermore disdain
   A Rival on my Throne.
He either fears his Fate too much,
   Or his Deserts are small,
That puts it not unto the Touch,
   To win or lose it all. ...

But if thou wilt be constant then,
   And faithful of thy Word,
I'll make thee glorious by my Pen,
   And famous by my Sword.
I'll serve thee in such noble Ways
   Was never heard before:
I'll crown and deck thee all with Bays,
   And love thee evermore.

71

IN MY COUNTRY

Jackie Kay   b. 1961

walking by the waters
down where an honest river
shakes hands with the sea,
a woman passed round me
in a slow watchful circle,
as if I were a superstition;

or the worst dregs of her imagination,
so when she finally spoke
her words spliced into bars
of an old wheel A segment of air.
Where do you come from?
'Here,' I said, 'Here. These parts.'

72

THE SPIK O' THE LAN

Sheena Blackhall b. 1947

The clash o' the kintra claik
Rins aff ma lug, as rain
Teems ower the glaissy gape
O' the windae pane.

The chap o' the preacher's wird,
Be it wise as Solomon,
It fooners on iron yird
Brakks, upon barren grun.

Bit the lowe o' a beast new born,
The grieve at his wirk,
The blyter o' brierin corn,
The bicker o' birk
The haly hush o' the hill:
Things kent, an at haun
I'd harken tae that wi' a will.
The Spik o' the lan!

TUNDRA'S EDGE

John Burnside b. 1955

Here is the wolf. The wind, the sound of rain,
the kitchen light that falls across the lawn –
these things are his. This house is his domain.

Here is the wolf. He slips in with the dawn
to raid your mirrors. Shadows will persist
for days, to mark the distance he has gone

in search of you. Yet still you will insist
the wolf died out in these parts long ago:
everyone knows the wolf does not exist.

You catch no scent. And where the mirrors glow
those are not eyes, but random sparks of light.
You never dream of running with the snow.

Yet here is Wolf. He rustles in the night.
Only the wind, but you switch on the light.

74

THE WATERGAW

Hugh MacDiarmid 1892–1978

Ae weet forenicht i' the yow-trummle
I saw yon antrin thing,
A watergaw wi' its chitterin licht
Ayont the on-ding;
An' I thocht o' the last wild look ye gied
Afore ye deed!

There was nae reek i' the laverock's hoose
That nicht – an' nane i' mine;
But I hae thocht o' that foolish licht
Ever sin' syne;
An' I think that mebbe at last I ken
What your look meant then.

WARMING HER PEARLS

Carol Ann Duffy b. 1955

For Judith Radstone

Next to my own skin, her pearls. My mistress
bids me wear them, warm them, until evening
when I'll brush her hair. At six, I place them
round her cool, white throat. All day I think of her,

resting in the Yellow Room, contemplating silk
or taffeta, which gown tonight? She fans herself
whilst I work willingly, my slow heat entering
each pearl. Slack on my neck, her rope.

She's beautiful. I dream about her
in my attic bed; picture her dancing
with tall men, puzzled by my faint, persistent scent
beneath her French perfume, her milky stones.

I dust her shoulders with a rabbit's foot,
watch the soft blush seep through her skin
like an indolent sigh. In her looking-glass
my red lips part as though I want to speak.

Full moon. Her carriage brings her home. I see
her every movement in my head. . . . Undressing,
taking off her jewels, her slim hand reaching
for the case, slipping naked into bed, the way

she always does. . . . And I lie here awake,
knowing the pearls are cooling even now
in the room where my mistress sleeps. All night
I feel their absence and I burn.

THE MAID'S ROOM

Dilys Rose b. 1954

No one sleeps there now but every visitor
is hustled up the narrow, grumbling staircase.
By torch or candlelight, shadows leap and twist.
Voices drop to whispers. The room is small,
spartan, impersonal. The single bed, the cold stove.
A gable window overlooks the minister's hedge.
How did she pass the hours when work was done –
toasting her toes, writing neat, heartsick letters
to a fiancé, exploring the map of Paris
he gave her the day his call-up papers came,
tracing *rues* and *boulevards* with chapped fingers,
names dissolving on her tongue like *petits fours*.
Champs Élysées. Bastille. Sacré Coeur.
Perhaps she read romances, train timetables,
crossed days off the calendar since war
stole her future, nursed embers in the grate
as if they were her hoped-for sleeping bairns.
And later, quilt pressed to her ears, prayed
that sleep would take her, swift as a train,
and that the master wouldn't require anything
extra. Then the hand bell. The dark stairs.

77

THE WORLD IS BUSY, KATIE

Richard Price b. 1966

The world is busy, Katie, and tonight
the planes are playing, fine, alright, but soon
the folk behind those blinks will nap, sleep tight,
as you will too, beneath a nitelite moon.
The world is busy, Katie, but it's late –
the trains are packing up, the drunks are calm.
The fast, the slow, has gone. It's only freight
that storms the garage lane. It means no harm.
The world is busy, Katie, but it's dark –
the lorries nod, they snort, they spoil their chrome.
They hate to be alone. For them, a lay-by's home.
The world is busy, Katie, like I said,
but *you're* the world – and tired. It's time for bed.

CAKE

Helena Nelson b. 1953

Bake a cake for a visitor.
The baker is wearing a rose-bud apron.
Her hair and hands are dusted with flour.

Eggs are waiting beside the cooker;
the butter and sugar are beaten to foam;
the wooden spoon is charged with power.

This is a cake descended of cakes
born in small ovens for generations,
a cake of fragrance and careful making.

A hint of almond is for forgiveness;
the soft lemon curd is for contrition;
vanilla summons the shade of sweetness.

The crumb of the cake will be pale and warm;
the scent of the cake will be clear as dawn;
the shape of the cake a golden sun.

It will rise, like heaven, and then be gone.

THE JEELIE PIECE SONG

Adam McNaughtan b. 1939

I'm a skyscraper wean, Ah live on the nineteenth flair,
But Ah'm no gaun oot tae play ony mair,
'Cause since we moved tae Castlemilk, Ah'm wastin'
    away
'Cause Ah'm getting' wan meal less every day.

Chorus
Oh ye cannae fling pieces oot a twinty-storey flat,
Seven hundred hungry weans'll testify to that.
If it's butter, cheese or jeelie, if the breid is plain or pan
The odds against it reachin' earth are ninety-nine to wan.

On the first day ma maw flung oot a daud o Hovis
    broon;
It cam skytin oot the windae and went up insteid o doon.
Noo every twinty-seven 'oors it comes back intae sight,
'Cause ma piece went intae orbit an' became a satellite.

On the next day ma maw flung me a piece oot wance
    again.
It went and hut the pilot in a fast low-flying plane.
He scraped it aff his goggles, shouting through the
    intercom,
'The Clydeside Reds've goat me wi a breid-an-jeelie bomb.'

On the third day ma maw thought she would try anither
   throw.
The Salvation Army baun' was staunin' doon below.
'Onward, Christian Soldiers' was the piece they should've
   played
But the oompah man was playin' a piece on
   marmalade.

We've wrote away tae Oxfam to try an' get some aid,
An' a' the weans in Castlemilk have formed a 'piece
   brigade'.
We're gonnae march to George's Square demandin' civil
   rights,
Like nae mair hooses ower piece-flinging height.

80

LAMENT FOR A LOST DINNER TICKET

Margaret Hamilton 1915–1972

See ma mammy
See ma dinner ticket
A pititnma
Pokit an she pititny
Washnmachine.

See thon burnty
Up wherra firewiz
Ma mammy says Am no tellnyagain
No'y playnit.
A jist wen'y eatma
Pokacrisps furma dinner
Nabigwoffldoon.

The wummin sed Aver near
Clapsd
Jistur heednur
Wee wellies sticknoot.

They sed Wot heppind?
Nme'nma belly
Na bedna hospital.
A sed A pititnma
Pokit an she pititny
Washnmachine.

They sed Ees thees chaild eb slootly
Non verbal ?
A sed MA BUMSAIR
    Nwen'y sleep.

burnty: burned-out house

81

Donny O'Rourke b. 1959

Your custom, often
when the house was still

to brew milky coffee
and reminisce.

Child care experts would have frowned
on my late hours,

the bitter adult drinks
and frothy confidences.

Yet your stories stopped my mewling
and continued as I grew

me tending the fire,
you talking of Ireland,

more real to your first born
than the younger ones who slept.

Those nightcaps, Mother,
were our hushed bond.

And though, for twenty years now,
I've drunk my coffee black,

I'm not weaned yet
of that rich, warm milk.

82

THE MOTHER

Joseph Lee 1876–1949

'Mother o' mine; O Mother o' mine.'

My mother rose from her grave last night,
    And bent above my bed,
And laid a warm kiss upon my lips,
    A cool hand on my head;
And 'Come to me, and come to me,
    My bonnie boy,' she said.

* * *

And when they found him at the dawn,
    His brow with blood defiled,
And gently laid him in the earth
    They wondered that he smiled.

83

HALLAIG

Somhairle MacGill-Eain *1911–1996*

'Tha tìm, am fiadh, an coille Hallaig'

Tha bùird is tàirnean air an uinneig
troimh 'm faca mi an Aird an Iar
's tha mo ghaol aig Allt Hallaig
'na craoibh bheithe, 's bha i riamh

eadar an t-Inbhir 's Poll a' Bhainne,
thall 's a bhos mu Bhaile-Chùirn:
tha i 'na beithe,'na calltuinn,
'na caorunn dhìreach shearng ùir.

Ann an Screapadal mo chinnidh,
far robh Tarmad 's Eachann Mór,
tha 'n nigheanan 's am mic 'nan coille
a' gabhail suas ri taobh an lóin.

Uaibhreach a nochd na coilich ghiuthais
a' gairm air mullach Cnoc an Rà,
dìreach an druim ris a' ghealaich –
chan iadsan coille mo ghràidh.

Fuirichidh mi ris a' bheithe
gus an tig i mach an Càrn,
gus am bi am bearradh uile
o Bheinn na Lice f' a sgàil.

Mura tig 's ann theàrnas mi a Hallaig,
a dh'ionnsaigh sàbaid nam marbh,
far a bheil an sluagh a' tathaich,
gach aon ghinealach a dh'fhalbh.

Tha iad fhathast ann a Hallaig,
Clann Ghill-Eain 's Clann MhicLeòid,
na bh' ann ri linn Mhic Ghille Chaluim:
chunnacas na mairbh beò.

Na fir 'nan laighe air an lianaig
aig ceann gach taighe a bh' ann,
na h-igheanan 'nan coille bheithe,
dìreach an druim, crom an ceann.

Eadar an Leac is na Feàrnaibh
tha 'n rathad mór fo chóinnich chiùin,
's na h-igheanan 'nam badan sàmhach
a' dol a Chlachan mar o thùs.

Agus a' tilleadh às a' Chlachan,
à Suidhisnis 's á tìr nam beò;
a chuile té òg uallach,
gun bhristeadh cridhe an sgeòil.

O Allt na Feàrnaibh gus an fhaoilinn
tha soilleir an dìomhaireachd nam beann
chan eil ach coimhthional nan nighean
a' cumail na coiseachd gun cheann.

A' tilleadh a Hallaig anns an fheasgar,
anns a' chamhanaich bhalbh bheò,
a' lìonadh nan leathadan casa,
an gàireachdaich 'nam chluais 'na ceò,

's am bòidhche 'na sgleò air mo chridhe
mun tig an ciaradh air na caoil,
's nuair theàrnas grian air cùl Dhùn Cana
thig peileir dian á gunna Ghaoil;

's buailear am fiadh a tha 'na thuaineal
a' snòtach nan làraichean feòir;
thig reothadh air a shùil 's a' choille:
chan fhaighear lorg air fhuil ri m' bheò.

HALLAIG

(translation)

Sorley Maclean 1911–1996

'Time, the deer, is in the wood of Hallaig'

The window is nailed and boarded
through which I saw the West
and my love is at the Burn of Hallaig,
a birch tree, and she has always been

between Inver and Milk Hollow,
here and there about Baile-chuirn:
she is a birch, a hazel,
a straight, slender young rowan.

In Screapadal of my people
where Norman and Big Hector were,
their daughters and their sons are a wood
going up beside the stream.

Proud tonight the pine cocks
crowing on the top of Cnoc an Ra,
straight their backs in the moonlight –
they are not the wood I love.

I will wait for the birch wood
until it comes up by the cairn,
until the whole ridge from Beinn na Lice
will be under its shade.

If it does not, I will go down to Hallaig,
to the Sabbath of the dead,
where the people are frequenting,
every single generation gone.

They are still in Hallaig,
MacLeans and MacLeods,
all who were there in the time of Mac Gille Chaluim:
the dead have been seen alive.

The men lying on the green
at the end of every house that was,
the girls a wood of birches,
straight their backs, bent their heads.

Between the Leac and Fearns
the road is under mild moss
and the girls in silent bands
go to Clachan as in the beginning,

and return from Clachan,
from Suisnish and the land of the living;
each one young and light-stepping,
without the heartbreak of the tale.

From the Burn of Fearns to the raised beach
that is clear in the mystery of the hills,
there is only the congregation of the girls
keeping up the endless walk,

coming back to Hallaig in the evening,
in the dumb living twilight,
filling the steep slopes,
their laughter a mist in my ears,

and their beauty a film on my heart
before the dimness comes on the kyles,
and when the sun goes down behind Dun Cana
a vehement bullet will come from the gun of Love;

and will strike the deer that goes dizzily,
sniffing at the grass-grown ruined homes;
his eye will freeze in the wood,
his blood will not be traced while I live.

84

TIMETABLE

Kate Clanchy b. 1965

We all remember school, of course:
the lino warming, shoe bag smell, expanse
of polished floor. It's where we learned
to wait: hot cheeked in class, dreaming,
bored, for cheesy milk, for noisy now.
We learned to count, to rule off days,
and pattern time in coloured squares:
purple English, dark green Maths.

We hear the bells, sometimes,
for years, the squeal and crack
of chalk on black. We walk, don't run,
in awkward pairs, hoping for the open door,
a foreign teacher, fire drill. And love
is long aertex summers, tennis sweat,
and somewhere, someone singing flat.
The art room, empty, full of light.

85

THE TWO SISTERS

Anon

There were twa sisters lived in a bower
   Binnorie, O Binnorie!
There came a knicht to be their wooer,
   By the bonnie mill-dams of Binnorie.

He courted the eldest with glove and ring;
But he loved the youngest aboon a' thing.

He courted the eldest with brooch and knife;
But he loved the youngest as his life.

The eldest she was vexèd sair,
And sair envied her sister fair.

Intil her bow'r she cou'dna rest;
With grief and spite she almus brast.

Upon a mornin' fair and clear,
She cried upon her sister dear:

'Oh, sister! come to the sea-strand,
And see our father's ships come to land.'

She's ta'en her by the milk-white hand,
And lad her down to yon sea-strand.

The youngest stood upon a stane,
The eldest came and pushed her in.

She took her by the middle sma',
And dash'd her bonnie back to the jaw.

'O sister, sister, reach your hand,
And ye shall be heir of half my land.'

'O sister, I'll not reach my hand,
And I'll be heir of all your land.' ...

'O sister, reach me but your glove,
And sweet William shall be your love.'

'Sink on, nor hope for hand or glove,
And sweet William shall better be my love.

'Your cherry cheeks, and your yellow hair,
Gar'd me gang maiden evermair.'

Sometimes she sunk, sometimes she swam,
Until she came to the miller's dam.

Oh, out it came the miller's son,
And saw the fair maid floating down.

'O father, father, draw your dam
   Binnorie, O Binnorie!
There's a mermaid or a milk-white swan
   In the bonnie mill-dams of Binnorie.'

The miller quickly drew the dam,
and there he found a drownd woman.

You cou'dna see her yellow hair,
For gowd and pearl that were so rare.

You cou'dna see her middle sma',
For her gowden girdle sae braw.

You cou'dna see her fingers white,
For gowden rings that were sae bright.

By there came a harper fine,
That harpèd to the king at dine.

And when he lookt that ladye on,
He sighed, and made a heavy moan …

He made a harp of her breast-bone,
Whose sounds would melt a heart of stone.

He's ta'en three locks of her yellow hair,
And with them strung his harp sae fair.

He brought the harp to her father's hall;
And there was the court assembled all.

He laid the harp upon a stane,
And straight it began to play alane.

'Oh, yonder sits my father, the king,
And yonder sits my mother, the queen.

But the last tune that the harp played then,
Was – 'Woe to my sister, false Helen!'

jaw: wave

86

CRABS: TIREE

Tom Pow b. 1950

We tied a worm of bacon fat
to a flat rock with string
and dropped it over the edge
into the clear water
of the bay. It fell gently

to the sand and the seaweed.
A tug told us we'd a bite
or we saw the crab itself
latch onto the ragged fat and pulled it
steadily out: this was the knack.

Too sudden, too sharp
and it dropped from its stone
shadow, so clumsily evading
its fate. But smoothly,
feeding the rough string

through fist upon fist
and they would come to us
like lumps of lava, water
sluicing from their backs.
Dumbly determined

they hung on
by one improbable claw
before the dull crack as they hit
the harbour wall, or the side
of the pails we kept them in.

Standing in a row,
four or five of us holiday kids
pulled out scores in a day, till each
bucket was a brackish mass
of fearsome crockery

bubbling below
its skin of salt water.
What happened to them all? –
our train of buckets, the great stench
of our summer sport.

It was a blond boy
from Glasgow finally pushed me in
head over heels from where
I crouched on the pier wall.
When I righted myself

I was waist deep in crab-
infested waters. No one
could pull me out. 'You must walk
to the shore,' my sister shouted
as I held my hands

high above my head,
thinking I could at least
save them. But how beautiful
it was all around me! The spatter
of green crofts

and deep blue lochans;
the cottontail; the buttercup
on the cropped foreshore. The sky
was depthless; all was silence.
And I was there

moving slowly through
this perfect blue wedge,
bearing terror in one hand, guilt
in the other, leaving the briefest wake
to mark my shame.

BEHIND YOUR EYES

Brian Johnstone b. 1950

There are times when you stop in your tracks,
halted by the scent of a blossom, the curve
of a particular leaf; times when these things

shift like the wind from absence to absence;
and all of you lurches forwards, foot before foot,
your mind one turn in the path from recognition

and this is one of these: a tree lies, particular of aspect,
along the way; a light blinks across the valley;
and darkness reaches out to touch you,

as this does, welling up from somewhere
you have been, you think, before but
did not know it, did not recognise the moment

that takes you now by something more
than just surprise; like something living, palpable,
that rustles in the underbrush, hides behind your eyes.

88

THE BEWTEIS OF THE FUTE-BALL

Anon

Brissit brawnis and broken banis,
Strife, discord and waistit wanis,
Crookit in eild, syne halt withal –
These are the bewteis of the fute-ball.

Brissit: burst, *wanis*: homes, *eild*: age

A FAIRY TALE

John Glenday b. 1952

She had been living happily ever before,
waltzing through imagined ballrooms in the arms
of a handsome young prince. Then, one day, they kiss
for the first time, he takes back the word love

and suddenly bloats to an idle, wounded beast
that stoops above her in its unfamiliar, thickening hide.
She trembles before his yellow breath and white, strange
    eyes.
Each night from her solitary bed, she overhears the
    echoes

of unimaginable rages which transform their castle
to a ruin of shadowy rooms with a cursed and sleeping
    heart.
At last she understands him poorly enough to be
    terrified
and run a gauntlet of scattering wolves to the arms of
    her sick father

who greets her with a tearful goodbye. They subsist
forever after on a diet of simple gruel and vague desire.
When passers-by ask her about her life, she waltzes the
    laundry
to her heart and answers with a distant smile: *Once upon
    a time.*

LERNIN

Alison Flett   b. 1965

thi wummin iz standin
by thi doar
the wee boy iz rite
inside thi shoap
thi man iz bitween
thi wummin
an thi boy

thi wee boy iz greetin
wi hiz hole body
thi wee shoodurz
shuddur
inside thi bobbly lookn
jumpur wi
sumthin sticky smujd
doon thi frunt
teerz make white scarz
throo thi muck
oan hiz crumply face

thi man goze
fukn MOOV
ah telt yi
moov it
NOW

thi wee laddy
greets hardur
mummy
he sayz
hiz arms reechin up
tay hur
mummy ah wont YOO
mummy PLEEZ

thi wummin
looks it thi boy
her eyebrows rinkul
hur body twitchiz
taywordz thi bairn
then she stops
looks it thi man

jist yoo stay
rite thare hen
he sayz
ahv telt yi bifore
dinny giv inty him
thi boyz goaty lern
yi heer mi?
thi boyz goaty lern

THE FREEDOM COME-ALL-YE

Hamish Henderson 1919–2002

Tune: The Bloody Fields of Flanders

Roch the wind in the clear day's dawin
    Blaws the cloods heelster-gowdie ow'r the bay,
But there's mair nor a roch wind blawin
    Through the great glen o' the warld the day.
It's a thocht that will gar oor rottans
      – A' they rogues that gang gallus, fresh and gay –
Tak the road, and seek ither loanins
    For their ill ploys, tae sport and play.

Nae mair will the bonnie callants
    Mairch tae war when oor braggarts crously craw,
Nor wee weans frae pit-heid and clachan
    Mourn the ships sailin' doon the Broomielaw.
Broken faimlies in lands we've herriet
    Will curse Scotland the Brave nae mair, nae mair;
Black and white, ane til ither mairriet,
    Mak the vile barracks o' their maisters bare.

So come all ye at hame wi' Freedom,
    Never heed whit the hoodies croak for doom.
In your hoose a' the bairns o' Adam
    Can find breid, barley-bree and painted room.
When Maclean meets wi's friens in Springburn,
    A' the roses and geans will turn tae bloom,
And a black boy frae yont Nyanga
    Dings the fell gallows o' the burghers doon.

92

CORPUS CHRISTI CAROL

James Hogg 1770–1835

The heron flew east, the heron flew west,
The heron flew to the fair forest;
She flew o'er streams and meadows green
And a' to see what could be seen:
And when she saw the faithful pair,
Her breast grew sick, her head grew sair;
For there she saw a lovely bower,
Was a' clad o'er wi' lilly-flower;
And in the bower there was a bed
With silken sheets, and weel down spread
And in the bed there lay a knight,
Whose wounds did bleed both day and night,
And by the bed there stood a stane,
And there was a' set a leal maiden,
With silver needle and silken thread,
Stemming the wounds when they did bleed.

93

THE QUEEN OF SHEBA

Kathleen Jamie b. 1962

Scotland, you have invoked her name
just once too often
in your Presbyterian living rooms.
She's heard, yea
even unto heathenish Arabia
your vixen's bark of poverty, come down
the family like a lang neb, a thrawn streak,
a wally dug you never liked
but can't get shot of.

She's had enough. She's come.
Whit, tae this dump? Yes!
She rides first camel
of a swaying caravan
from her desert sands
to the peat and bracken
of the Pentland hills
across the fit-ba pitch
to the thin mirage
of the swings and chute; scattered with glass.

Breathe that steamy musk
on the Curriehill Road, not mutton-shanks
boiled for broth, nor the chlorine stink
of the swimming pool where skinny girls
accuse each other of verrucas.
In her bathhouses women bear
warm pot-bellied terracotta pitchers
on their laughing hips.
All that she desires, whatever she asks
She will make the bottled dreams
of your wee lasses
look like *sweeties*.

Spangles scarcely cover
her gorgeous breasts, hanging gardens
jewels, frankincense; more voluptuous
even than Vi-next-door, whose
high-heeled slippers
keeked from dressing gowns
like little hooves, wee tails
of pink fur stuffed in the cleavage of her toes;
more audacious even than Currie Liz
who led the gala floats
through the Wimpey scheme
in a ruby-red Lotus Elan
before the Boys' Brigade band
and the Brownies' borrowed coal-truck;
hair piled like candy-floss;
who lifted her hands from the neat wheel
to tinkle her fingers
at her tricks
    among the Masons and the elders and the police.

The cool black skin
of the Bible couldn't hold her,
nor the atlas green
on the kitchen table,
you stuck with thumbs
and split to fruity hemispheres –
yellow Yemen, Red Sea, *Ethiopia*. Stick in
with the homework and you'll be
cliver like yer faither.
but no too cliver,
no *above yersel*.

See her lead those great soft camels
widdershins round the kirk-yaird,
smiling
as she eats
avocados with apostle spoons
she'll teach us how. But first

she wants to strip the willow
she desires the keys
    to the National Library
she is beckoning
    the lasses
    in the awestruck crowd...

Yes, we'd like to
         clap the camels,
to smell the spice,
admire her hairy legs and
bonny wicked smile, we want to take
PhDs in Persian, be vice
to her president: we want
to help her
         ask some Difficult Questions

she's shouting for our wisest man
to test her mettle:

         Scour Scotland for a Solomon!

Sure enough: from the back of the crowd
someone growls:

         whae do you think y'ur?

and a thousand laughing girls and she
draw our hot breath
         and shout:

THE QUEEN OF SHEBA!

94

George Bruce 1909–2002

Someone is waving a white handkerchief
from the train as it pulls out with a white
plume from the station and rumbles its way
to somewhere that does not matter. But
it will pass the white sands and the broad sea
that I have watched under the sun and moon
in the stop of time in my childhood as I am
now there again and waiting for the white
handkerchief. I shall not see her again
but the waters rise and fall and the horizon
is firm. You who have not seen that line
hold the brimming sea to the round earth
cannot know this pain and sweetness of departure.

95

CAPERNAUM

Lewis Spence 1874–1955

Matthew xi, 23

If aa the bluid shed at thy Tron,
Embro, Embro,
If aa the bluid shed at thy Tron
Were sped into a river,
It wad caa the mills o Bonnington,
Embro, Embro,
It wad caa the mills o Bonnington
For ever and for ever.

If aa the tears that thou has grat,
Embro, Embro,
If aa the tears that thou has grat
Were shed into the sea,
Whaur wad ye find an Ararat,
Embro, Embro,
Whaur wad ye find an Ararat
Frae that fell flude to flee?

If aa the psalms sung in thy kirks,
Embro, Embro,
If aa the psalms sung in thy kirks
Were gaithered in a wind,
It wad shog the taps o Roslin birks,
Embro, Embro,
It wad shog the taps o Roslin birks
Till time was out o mynd.

If aa the broken herts o thee,
Embro, Embro,
If aa the broken herts o thee
Were heapit in a howe,
There wad be neither land nor sea,
Embro, Embro,
There wad be neither land nor sea
But yon reid brae – and thou!

caa: keep in motion; *shog*: shake

96

HAYMARKET SUNSET

Angus Calder b. 1942

For Sandy Robb

That lass in a woolly cap with earflaps
waiting at dusk for a bus by Haymarket Station
may conceivably have mince for brains
but at least her delicate profile and clear eyes
suggest potential. The young have not yet
been defeated, their gaze is towards tomorrow,
their step is forward. I stare back over decades –
so many times at this bus-stop as sunset,
salmon and jade, has ebbed behind Corstorphine.
As I ride out once again to curling, my
tomorrows are fewer. However, week by week,
even hour by hour, Murrayfield ice is always
different. You have to adjust your weight,
your line, your sweep. And this light is always beautiful.

97

Alexander Hume 1556–1609

...The gloming comes, the day is spent,
The sun goes out of sight,
And painted is the Occident
With pourpour sanguine bright.

The skarlet nor the golden threid,
Who would their beawtie trie,
Are nathing like the colour reid
And beautie of the sky.

Our west horizon circuler,
Fra time the sunne be set,
Is all with rubies (as it wer)
Or rosis reid ou'rfret.

What pleasour were to waike and see,
Endlang a river cleare,
The perfite forme of everie tree
Within the deepe appeare!

The salmon out of cruifs and creils
Up hailed into skowts,
The bels and circles on the weills,
Throw lowpping of the trouts.

O then it were a seemely thing,
While all is still and calme,
The praise of God to play and sing,
With cornet and with shalme.

Bot now the birds with mony schout
Cals uther be their name:
'Ga, Billie, turne our gude about,
Now time is to go hame.'

With bellie fow the beastes belive
Are turned fra the come,
Quhilk soberly they hameward drive,
With pipe and lilting horne.

Throw all the land great is the gild
Of rustik folk that crie,
Of bleiting sheep fra they be fild,
Of calves and rowting ky.

All labourers drawes hame at even,
And can till uther say,
Thankes to the gracious God of heaven,
Quhilk send this summer day.

ou'rfret: embroidered; *bels*: bubbles; *weills*: pools; *shalme*:
shawm (an oboe-like instrument); *gude*: livestock; *belive*:
quickly; *gild*: clamour; *send*: sent

98

THE FLY-TIER'S DREAM

Norman Kreitman b. 1927

Hunched like one of Alberich's dwarfs
he bent over the clutter
of pelts and capes by the elegant vice,
the scatter of bobbins, spindles, thread.

His intelligent fingers turned, turned.
In his ear variations of sainted names –
*Greenwell's Glory, Teal and Green,
Kingfisher Butcher, Bibio, Tupp's.*

But the lordly salmon and preoccupied trout
were alike indifferent to his craft.
So back to the bench, deep thought.
Then a vision came into his eye

of an art that aspired to more gorgeous hues –
vermilion on black, sulphur yellow
with touches of white, and behind the fat hook
a tuft of rainbow tinsel. An angelic confection.

Useless, of course, for our homely river
fretting with problems of eddies and silt,
but perfect for the great pearly fish
swimming four abreast in the waters of Heaven.

99

TO S.R. CROCKETT

Robert Louis Stevenson 1850–1894

Blows the wind to-day, and the sun and the rain are flying,
Blows the wind on the moors to-day and now,
Where about the graves of the martyrs the whaups are
  crying,
My heart remembers how!

Grey recumbent tombs of the dead in desert places,
Standing Stones on the vacant wine-red moor,
Hills of sheep, and the howes of the silent vanished
  races,
And winds, austere and pure!

Be it granted me to behold you again in dying,
Hills of home! and to hear again the call;
Hear about the graves of the martyrs the peewees crying;
And hear no more at all.

100

THE BIG HOOLEY

Nancy Somerville b. 1953

1st July 1999

In the Assembly Rooms thenight,
people want tae dance, an celebrate.
The hall swirls tae the Fish Band,
kilts, skirts, troosers, shorts,
even the odd ball gown
twirlin an birlin in time tae the music
lik a shoal turnin as wan
in the ocean's currents.

Ah've jist danced wi an msp;
Hell, evrybuddy in the room huz,
an Ah'm thinkin ae auld Edinburgh
n'how aw the classes
yaised tae live'n work'n eat
cheek bi jowl,
crammed alang the spine ae the auld toon,

n'Ah think ae ma sons
n'the rest ae their generation
doon in the Gerdens
listnin tae Shirley Manson an Garbage
n'Ah know they'll be huvvin
jist as good a time as Ah um,
n'Ah know they can ceilidh
wi the best ae thum,

furr this country isnae wan culture,
ur class,
wurr no wan generation,
ur gender,
wiv goat merr than wan language,
an strings tae wur bow,
wur each ai us bitsae awthings,
wi as many moods'n aspects
as the weather,

an as lang as we remember
tae celebrate that,
wull be fine.

NOTES

1   **ROBERT BURNS** was born in Alloway, Ayrshire, the son of a tenant-farmer. On his father's death, he and his brother Gilbert took on the ailing farm of Mossgeil near Mauchline. 1786 saw the early flowering of his genius, the Kilmarnock edition of *Poems, Chiefly in the Scottish Dialect.* Despite the blandishments of the Edinburgh literati, he stuck to the rural vernacular which energised his lyrics and the traditional songs he recrafted. In 1788 he married Jean Armour. Further farming attempts failing, he joined the Excise in Dumfries where, plagued by money troubles and ill-health, he died aged thirty-seven. The rousing radicalism and egalitarian sentiments of 'A Man's a Man' (1795) bear witness to the impact on him of the French Revolution.

2   **DOUGLAS DUNN** was born and grew up in Inchinnan, in Renfrewshire. 'Landscape with One Figure' is set there, on the south bank of the Clyde, opposite what used to be John Brown's shipyard. He has published ten collections of poetry plus his *New Selected Poems* (2003), in conjunction with critical works, and volumes of stories. He edited *The Faber Book of Twentieth Century Scottish Poetry* (1992) and *The Oxford Book of Scottish Short Stories* (1995). He works as a Professor of English at the University of St Andrews, having founded the postgraduate M.Litt in Creative Writing in 1993.

3   **ALASTAIR REID**, born in Whithorn, graduated from the University of St Andrews after war service in the navy. He has lived in Europe, the United States, and Central and South America. For many years a staff

writer with *The New Yorker,* he is highly regarded as an essayist and translator, and especially for his English versions of Neruda and Borges, both of whom he knew. *Weathering* appeared in 1978, and *Oases* in 1999. In 1984 he built a house on a remote peninsula in the Dominican Republic near where Columbus landed on his first voyage of discovery and called in his log 'the fairest ever looked on by human eyes'.

4　**ANON** 'The Bonnie Earl of Moray'　In 1592 James VI, jealous at his Queen having rashly commended James Stewart, Earl of Moray, believed to have been associated with the Earl of Bothwell in an assault on Holyrood, ordered his murder. The dying man, struck in the face by Huntly, upbraided him with 'having spoilt a better face than his own'.

5　**ANON** 'Memorial of St Columba' (translated by Gilbert Márkus) This devotional piece ('Os mutorum…'), casting Columba as patron of the nation, is from the late 13th or early 14th century *Inchcolm Antiphoner*: one of the most important manuscripts in the history of plainchant, it contains the only definitive remnants of the music of the Celtic church.

6　**JOHN PURSER** was born in Glasgow. He has published three collections of poetry. He is also known as a composer and author of radio plays, including 'Carver'. His book and radio series *Scotland's Music* won the McVitie Scottish Writer of the Year Award and a Sony Gold Medal, respectively. He lives and crofts on the Isle of Skye. His poem on St Columba is one of a series of 'Dialogues Concerning Natural Religion' (its title from the great Scottish philosopher, David Hume) exploring the interaction of faith and rationality.

7   **ROBERT CRAWFORD** was born and grew up in Lanarkshire. He likes to think of Scotland, like China, as a soup culture, and wanted to add to the menu of Scottish food poems. 'Turnipocephalic' is English for 'neip-heidit'. Crawford writes in English and Scots, and sometimes stir-fries mixtures of the two. His *Selected Poems* was published in 2005. With Mick Imlah he edited *The New Penguin Book of Scottish Verse* (2000), and he is completing *The Penguin History of Scottish Literature*. He is Professor of Modern Scottish Literature at St Andrews University.

8   **JOHN M. CAIE**, a son of the manse, was born near Banchory. After studying at Aberdeen University and the North of Scotland College of Agriculture, he lectured in Ireland and Scotland before becoming a senior civil servant in the Department of Agriculture. His rural roots, and an ear for local speech, mark *The Kindly North: Verse in Scots and English* (1934) and *'Twixt Hills and Sea* (1939).

9   **RON BUTLIN** has held writer's residences, and won awards, here and abroad. His novels *The Sound of my Voice* and *Belonging* were published in 1987 and 2006 respectively, and *No More Angels* (short stories) is due in 2007. A regular contributor to the *Sunday Herald* and the *TLS*, he lives in Edinburgh with his wife, the writer Regi Claire. The setting of 'At Linton Kirk' (from *Without a Backward Glance: New and Selected Poems,* 2005) is that of one of the oldest and most picturesque churches in Scotland, just outside Kelso.

10 **ALICIA SPOTTISWOODE** (Lady John Scott) This moving expression of love and loss, imbued with a sense of place, is from *Songs and Verses* (1904), published four years after she died, having been forty years a

widow. A staunch Jacobite, and an early collector of folk music, her reputation as a composer rests primarily on her version of 'Annie Laurie'.

11 **GEORGE MACKAY BROWN** was born in Stromness, the 'Hamnavoe' of his poems and stories. After studying at Newbattle College and Edinburgh University, he rarely left Orkney. His poetry, steeped in the history, culture and ritual of the islands, reveals his devotion to them – and to his craft. Among his many publications are *The Calendar of Love* and *A Time to Keep* (stories), *Magnus* and *Greenvoe* (novels), an autobiography *For the Islands I Sing*, and fourteen collections of poems. The *Collected Poems* was published posthumously in 2005.

12 **ANON** 'O Waly, Waly' Obscure in origin, it first appears in Allan Ramsay's *Tea-Table Miscellany* (1724). John Buchan, in his anthology of Scots vernacular poetry, *The Northern Muse*, describes it as 'the noblest of all the anonymous songs of Scotland'. It has been suggested however, that it was written in the late 1600s by Lady Barbara Erskine, on her desertion by her husband James, the second Marquis of Douglas.

13 **VALERIE GILLIES**, born in Canada, grew up in Scotland and was educated in Edinburgh and Mysore, India. She has held writing fellowships throughout Scotland, edited the first poetry map of Scotland, and was appointed Edinburgh's Makar in 2005. Her most recent collections are *Men and Beasts* (2000) and *The Lightning Tree* (2002). In 2005 she received a Creative Scotland Award to write 'The Spring Teller' – poems inspired by the springs and wells of Scotland and Ireland.

14 **CAROLINA OLIPHANT** was born in Gask, Perthshire. In 1806 she married a cousin, on whose restoration to

his forfeited estates and peerage she became Lady Nairne. They lived in Edinburgh until his death. In the 1820s, as 'Mrs Bogan of Bogan', she contributed Scots songs, many suffused with a genteel parlour Jacobitism, to *The Scottish Minstrelsy.*

15   **GERRY CAMBRIDGE** founded and edits *The Dark Horse*, a Scottish-American poetry magazine. From 1997 to 1999 he was Hugh MacDiarmid writing fellow at Brownsbank, Biggar. His most recent volume is *Madame Fi Fi's Farewell and Other Poems* (2003). 'A Winter Morning', based on memories as a teenager growing up in rural Ayrshire in the 1970s, is one of a group of poems in which he explores adolescence. His website is at www.gerrycambridge.com.

16   **GERALD MANGAN**, born in Glasgow, is a poet, playwright, journalist, painter and cartoonist, whose collections include *Waiting for the Storm* (1990). He has lived in Paris since 1987, reviewing and illustrating for the *TLS* and other journals. He says: 'I wrote "Ailsa Craig" after my father died in 1984, of sudden heart-failure. I was sure that his lifelong anger and frustration had contributed to his death, and I was remembering a night of my childhood, during a holiday in the Ayrshire village of Maidens, when he really allowed it all to show.'

17   **ANON** 'Sir Patrick Spens' This 'grand old ballad' as Coleridge styled it is among those purportedly based on historical fact. Claims linking it with a specific reign or circumstance, such as James III's marriage to the 'Maid of Norway', however, remain dubious. In this longer version, favoured by Walter Scott, the trappings of human vanity are set graphically against the tragic loss of the vessel and its crew.

18 **IAIN CRICHTON SMITH** / *Iain Mac A' Gobhainn* was born in Glasgow, and brought up on the Isle of Lewis. Educated in Stornoway and at Aberdeen University, he was a teacher in Clydebank and Oban, before resigning in 1977 to write full-time. His output, comprising poetry, novels, stories and plays was prolific, in both English and Gaelic. Subsequent to his *Collected Poems* of 1992 were *The Leaf and the Marble* (1998) and *A Country for Old Men* (2000). His complete short stories and 'Murdo' works also appeared posthumously, in 2001. 'Luss Village' is from the formally elegant early volume *Thistles and Roses* (1961).

19 **TESSA RANSFORD**, born in India, formed the School of Poets (1981), and founded and was the first director of the Scottish Poetry Library. From 1988 to 1998 she edited *Lines Review*, published by her husband Callum Macdonald, in whose memory she inaugurated an annual pamphlet award. She was elected president of Scottish PEN in 2004. Her poem's contrast between the natural river and the artificial pool illustrates our separation from nature: 'To lead one another, as if blind, is another way of surrendering to immanence, even within the unnatural "street".'

20 **ANNA CROWE**, a poet and translator, has since 1986 lived in St Andrews, where she co-founded StAnza, Scotland's Poetry Festival. Publications include *Skating out of the House* (1997) and *Punk with Dulcimer* (2006). Forthcoming are *Tugs in the Fog*, translations of poems by the Catalan writer Joan Margarit and an anthology of Catalan poetry in translation. 'Gollop's' looks back to childhood visits to grandparents in Plymouth, and is dedicated to her sister, Rosy, who died in 2004.

21 **MARION ANGUS** grew up in Arbroath where her father

was a United Presbyterian Kirk minister, and lived most of her life in Aberdeen. She began to write poetry in her fifties. Most of her lyrics, in Angus Scots and influenced by Scottish folk song and the ballads, ranged around what she termed 'the cauld east countra'. A forerunner of the upsurge of writing in Scots, she was represented in Hugh MacDiarmid's *Northern Numbers* (1921–2). Her *Selected Poems* were published in 1950 and she shares a selection with Violet Jacob in *Voices from Their Ain Countrie* (2006).

22 **JANET PAISLEY** is an award-winning poet, playwright, and fiction and script-writer. Her poetry collections include *Alien Crop* (1996), *Reading the Bones* (1999), and *Ye Cannae Win* (2000). Her short stories *Not for Glory* were published in 2001; and her most recent publication is the Sandstone Press novella *Wicked!*. She writes in Scots and English. The poem, 'Sarah: Fed Up', was written for the BBC series 'Around Scotland'.

23 **ANON** 'Macpherson's Rant' In 1700 James Macpherson, a Speyside gypsy fiddler, was hanged for theft at the Cross at Banff – a girl he loved having supposedly been used as bait to lure him into a trap. By the time news of a reprieve arrived it was too late – through the deliberate advancing, legend has it, of the town clock. His broken fiddle is preserved in the Clan Macpherson museum at Newtonmore.

24 **ROBERT GARIOCH** (Sutherland) read English at Edinburgh University. His war service in North Africa included a spell as a prisoner of war, which was the impetus for his poem 'The Wire'. Taking early retirement from teaching, he worked in The School of Scottish Studies, mainly, in his own words, as 'a lexicographer's orraman'. His impeccable craftsmanship is evident,

from 'Embro to the Ploy' and versions of the 19th century Roman poet Belli, to his *Edinburgh Sonnets,* which catch the rhythms of the city. His *Complete Poetical Works* were published in 1983.

25 **VIOLET JACOB** was born at the House of Dun, her family's home near Montrose. After marriage to an army officer she lived in India and the south of England, before returning to Angus. She wrote fiction for adults and children, and verse, in English. In her poetry in Scots, her ear is attuned to the dialect of her native region. Her *Songs of Angus* (1915, 1918) pre-dated MacDiarmid, to whose *Northern Numbers* anthologies she contributed when he was still writing in English. A selection of her poems along with those of Marion Angus is published as *Voices from Their Ain Countrie* (2006). Her only son was killed at the Battle of the Somme in 1916.

26 **SIR ALEXANDER GRAY**, born and schooled in Dundee, studied at the Universities of Edinburgh, Göttingen and Paris. After a spell in the Civil Service, he became professor of political economy in Aberdeen and Edinburgh. He drew on North-East Scots both in his own poems and as a basis for his copious translations of ballads and folk-songs, principally from Scandinavia and Germany.

27 **STEPHEN MULRINE** was born in Glasgow. A former lecturer at Glasgow School of Art, he has also taught creative writing, and his own work ranges from poetry and short stories to television and radio plays, serials and adaptations. Since 1988 he has concentrated on translation, chiefly from Russian, including plays by Gogol, Turgenev and Chekhov, and by contemporary writers. His 'The Coming of the Wee Malkies', fre-

quently read in schools, is sometimes described as a 'Friday afternoon' poem, perhaps because it tends to encourage a copycat spirit of anarchy.

28 LIZ LOCHHEAD, from Lanarkshire, was educated at Glasgow School of Art. Among her collections of poetry are *Dreaming Frankenstein* (1983) and *The Colour of Black & White* (2003). Her stage plays include *Blood and Ice, Mary Queen of Scots Got Her Head Chopped Off, Perfect Days*; adaptations of *Tartuffe* and (from *Le Misanthrope*) *Miserygut, Medea* and *Thebans*. She became Glasgow's Poet Laureate in 2005. This poem is for New Year, and the anniversary of their first meeting, for her then-brand-new husband, Tom. She's sure that only the ubiquitous, imperative Hogmanay and Ne'erdy customs and rituals it details let it make much sense to anyone else.

29 SIR WALTER SCOTT, born in Edinburgh and sickly as a child, was looked after by grandparents near Kelso. These years and the history, romances and balladry of the Borders had an enduring impact on his life and writing – from the towering achievement of the Waverley novels and success of his long narrative poems, to his tenure as 'Shirra' of Selkirkshire and Clerk to the Court of Session in Edinburgh. He unearthed the long-lost Scottish regalia, and made an indelible contribution to Scotland's cultural identity. This poem might be called Madge Wildfire's song, after the tragic character in *The Heart of Midlothian* who, having lost her reason, sings it on her deathbed. Its plaintive delivery 'had something of the lulling sound with which a mother sings her infant asleep'.

30 ELIZABETH BURNS grew up in Edinburgh. Her poetry collections are *Ophelia* (1991) and *The Gift of Light*

(1999). The poem here is the final one in the latter volume, and ending the poem – and the book – with a dash rather than a full stop indicates the tentative, uncertain feeling of the period just before giving birth. A forthcoming collection, *The Lantern Bearers*, opens with a poem about the birth itself, and the child emerging into 'so much light'.

31 **GILLIAN K. FERGUSON** has a degree in Philosophy from Edinburgh University, and worked as jewellery-maker, artist, and Arts Tutor at the Open University, before journalism and television arts reviewing. Publications include *Air for Sleeping Fish* (1997) and *Baby: Poems on Pregnancy, Birth and Babies* (2001). She won a Creative Scotland Award to work on 'The Human Genome: Poems on the Book of Life'. 'At the risk of sounding like an earth mother, when I had my Spring baby I felt enormously connected to nature, the new season: this poem is about how he seemed part of it all, and welcomed by nature.'

32 **JOE CORRIE** grew up in the mining community of Bowhill, in Fife. A miner himself until the 1920s, he then became a fulltime writer, forming and touring with the Bowhill Players. His prolific output, primarily for the amateur stage, brought popular success. His most powerful works were *Hewers of Coal* and *In Time of Strife*, the latter depicting the devastating effect of the 1926 General Strike on miners and their families. His poetry, too, reveals humanity and political fervour, and a belief in the dignity of the common man.

33 **ALEXANDER ANDERSON**, for a while a labourer on the railways, wrote poems on this theme under the name 'Surfaceman'. His output also included verses, of which the one here remains the best known, for young people.

34 **JEAN ELLIOT** was the third daughter of the second Baronet of Minto. She set this emotive piece, with its traditional opening and refrain, to a melody perhaps dating from before Flodden. First published anonymously in 1776, it was accepted by some (though not by Robert Burns) as genuinely from the 16th century, until traced to her. Her sole surviving composition, part of its appeal lies in the mystery of its origin.

35 **JAMES AITCHISON** was born in Stirlingshire and educated at Glasgow and Strathclyde Universities. He has published five collections of poems, most recently *Brain Scans* (1998) and *Bird-Score* (2002). His critical study *The Golden Harvester: The Vision Of Edwin Muir* appeared in 1988; and with Alexander Scott he edited the first three volumes *of New Writing Scotland*. This early poem was written while he and his wife were living for a short while in the village of Skinflats.

36 **JIM CARRUTH** was born in Johnstone and grew up on his family's farm near Kilbarchan. After a period in Turkey, he returned to live in Renfrewshire. His first collection, *Bovine Pastoral,* was published in 2004, and a second collection, *High Auchensale,* is due out in 2006. The poem 'The man who wanted to hug cows' explores themes of loss, acceptance and belonging.

37 **ROBERT FERGUSSON** was born in Edinburgh and educated there and in Dundee, and at the University of St Andrews. His early work was in English, but the poems on which his reputation rests are in a vibrant urban vernacular, which not only caught the flavour of contemporary Edinburgh but revived the literary potential of Scots. Illness and a fall were followed by his confinement in the Bedlam, where he died aged 24. His pauper's grave went unmarked until, thirteen

years later, a memorial was raised to him by Robert Burns – on whom he exerted a major influence. The extracts here, from the poem generally regarded as his masterpiece, graphically convey the flavour of the capital of his day.

38 **BRIAN MCCABE**, born in a small mining community near Edinburgh, studied Philosophy and English Literature at Edinburgh University, to which he was appointed Writer in Residence in 2005. His latest poetry collection is *Body Parts* (1999). His most recent volume of short stories, *A Date with My Wife* was published in 2001, and his *Selected Stories* in 2003. 'Seagull' was prompted by his waking early one Sunday, to hear the scavengers descending: he enjoys using different speakers in poems, and the challenge of imagining how a creature would use human language.

39 **CHARLES MURRAY** was born in Alford and trained as an engineer in Aberdeen. He worked for most of his life in the Transvaal, returning home on his retirement as Secretary of Public Works for the Union of South Africa. While abroad, he recalled the village community of his early days and its representative types. *Hamewith* (1909) made his reputation. At times he expresses a sardonic wit, and at others reflects the world of the ballads. 'The Whistle' and 'Gin I Were God', in particular, have been widely anthologised.

40 **CHARLES, LORD NEAVES**, born in Edinburgh into a legal family, became a judge in the Court of Session in 1854. A regular contributor to *Blackwood's Magazine,* his *Songs and Verses, Social and Scientific* went into several editions.

41 **TOM LEONARD** was born in Glasgow. His two collec-

tions of poetry, *Intimate Voices* and *access to the silence,* constitute his seminal *Collected Poems 1965–2004*. The author of critical essays and dramatic work, and a biography of James Thomson of Port Glasgow, *Places of the Mind: The Life and Work of James Thomson (B.V.),* he also compiled the anthology *Radical Renfrew: Poetry from the French Revolution to the First World War.* He teaches Creative Writing at Glasgow University. His website is at www.tomleonard.co.uk.

42 **W.S. GRAHAM** was born and brought up in Greenock, trained as an engineer and studied at Newbattle Abbey College. In 1943 he moved to Cornwall, and apart from two periods of teaching in New York, and regular visits abroad, lived there for the remainder of his life. After his early poems had attracted attention, he was taken on by T.S. Eliot, then editor at Faber who published all his subsequent volumes including *The White Threshold, The Nightfishing, Malcolm Mooney's Land,* and *Implements In Their Places*. A substantial *New Collected Poems* was published in 2004. *The Nightfisherman* (Carcanet) with his selected letters, many on poetry and the conundrums of language, appeared in 1999.

43 **W.D. COCKER** was born in Rutherglen into a family of Glasgow merchants. After the First World War he joined the accounts department of the *Daily Record*, whose amateur drama critic he was until he retired in 1956. His popular verse can be found in *Poems, Scots and English* (1932) and *Further Poems, Scots and English* (1935).

44 **HAMISH BROWN**, from a Fife family, has spent a lifetime mountain-climbing, trekking and wandering worldwide. His home is now Burntisland. A writer, lecturer and photographer, he has written, edited and

contributed to some thirty books including *The Bothy Brew* (stories), *Time Gentlemen* (collected poems), *Poems of the Scottish Hills*, and the outdoor classics *Hamish's Mountain Walk* and *Climbing the Corbetts.*

45 **ANDREW YOUNG**, priest, poet, topographer and naturalist, was born in Elgin. After studying at Edinburgh University and New College, Edinburgh he was ordained to the United Free Church, before moving to Sussex where he became successively an English Presbyterian minister and an Anglican vicar. He produced books on botany, history and folklore as well as poetry. He received the Queen's Gold Medal for Poetry in 1952. His *Selected Poems*, with wood engravings by Joan Hassall, were published in 1998.

46 **JAMES ROBERTSON**'s publications include the novels *The Fanatic* (2000), *Joseph Knight* (2003) and *The Testament of Gideon Mack* (2006), and the poetry collection *Sound-Shadow* (1996). 'A Manifesto for MSPs', which is in a fairly dense Scots – intended to make politicians and others read deeply, and to show the language's continuing relevance to the nation's cultural and political life – comes from a group of sonnets written as the outcome of his three-day residency at the Scottish Parliament in November 2004. These appear in *Voyage of Intent: Sonnets and Essays from the Scottish Parliament* (2005).

47 **MURIEL SPARK** was Edinburgh-born and educated. On moving to London she ran the Poetry Society and edited *The Poetry Review* 1947–49, before turning to the inimitable prose works – *The Prime of Miss Jean Brodie* (1961) remaining the best-known – which brought international recognition. Long resident in Tuscany, she was made a Dame in 1993. A volume of *Collected*

Poems was published in 1967, and *Going Up to Sotheby's* in 1982. Her foreword to *All the Poems* (2004) states: 'Although most of my life has been devoted to fiction, I have always thought of myself as a poet'.

48 **ANGELA MCSEVENEY** was brought up in Ross-shire, Livingstone and the Borders. In 1982 she moved to study in Edinburgh, where she now lives and works as a personal care assistant. Her latest collection is *Imprint* (2002). She read the relevant footnote while browsing in Edinburgh Central Library but, not realising it would one day inspire a poem, didn't note down the proper source. Initially incredulous, various unsolicited encounters in the street have made her wonder if perhaps Freud had a point...

49 **W.N. HERBERT** was born in Dundee. He now lives in North Shields and teaches Creative Writing at Newcastle University. He has published five collections of poetry, of which the most recent have been *The Laurelude* (1998), *The Big Bumper Book of Troy* (2002) and *Bad Shaman Blues* (2006). 'The Land o' Cakes', from the New Generation title *Forked Tongue* (1994), is a lament for a much-loved aunt and for the sweetness of the Scottish tooth.

50 **ALASDAIR MaCLEAN**, born in Glasgow, worked in the Clyde shipyards, did National Service at sea, and was a laboratory technician in Canada. Later he became a mature student in Edinburgh. His first collection of poems was *From the Wilderness* (1973). This and his subsequent volumes of both verse (*Waking the Dead, 1976*) and prose (*Night Falls in Ardnamurchan: The Twilight of a Crofting Family*) emphasised his close ties with the bleak finger of rock with which as a writer he identified. His poetry has a rigour consistent with his

claim, 'God was short of earth when He made Ardnamurchan'.

51 **NORMAN MacCAIG** was born in Edinburgh and educated at the Royal High School and Edinburgh University. A conscientious objector during the Second World War, he was for many years a primary school teacher. From *Riding Lights* (1955) to *Voice Over* (1988) he published fourteen collections of poetry. He was appointed Fellow in Creative Writing at Edinburgh in 1967, and in 1970 he became a Reader in poetry at the University of Stirling. He divided his life between Edinburgh and Lochinver, the landscape of the latter recurring in his poetry. The definitive *Poems of Norman MacCaig* was published in 2005.

52 **TOM BUCHAN** was born in Glasgow. He taught at Denny High School before becoming a lecturer at Madras University, India (1957–58). On returning to Scotland he continued to teach and lecture. A believer that 'the only possible role for the writer today is a subversive one', he published a novel and several plays as well as his poetry, which includes *Dolphins at Cochin* (1969) and *Poems 1969–1972*.

53 **WILLIAM SOUTAR** was born in Perth. In the 1920s he started to write in Scots for both adults and children. While in the Navy during the First World War, he contracted a form of spondylitis which led to ossification of the spine. Though bedridden for the last thirteen years of his life, his diaries and journals testify to an undiminished receptivity and openness to experience. *Into a Room: selected poems of William Soutar* appeared in 2000.

54 **EDWIN MORGAN** was born in Glasgow. He served with

the Royal Army Medical Corps 1940–46. He was Lecturer, and later Professor of English at Glasgow University until he retired in 1980. From 1999 to 2002 he was Glasgow's first Laureate, and in 2004 was appointed Scotland's National Poet. His prolific output, as eclectic as it is cosmopolitan, includes *Collected Poems* (1990), *Collected Translations* (1996), *New Selected Poems* (2000), *Cathures* (2002); as well as works of criticism and theatre versions of *Cyrano de Bergerac* and *Phèdre*. The comic-concrete and celebratory 'Canedolia' was in his 1968 volume *The Second Life*.

55 DON PATERSON was born and schooled in Dundee. In 1984 he moved to London to pursue a career in music; returning to Dundee as Writer in Residence to the University in 1993 – the year his first collection *Nil Nil* was published. There have followed *God's Gift to Women* (1997), *The Eyes* (1999) and *Landing Light* (2003). The only poet to have won the T.S. Eliot Prize twice, he lives in Kirriemuir, Angus. 'In the late 18th century a local seer, one Thomas Cairnie of Inchture, continually predicted the founding of a great kirk in the Carse of Gowrie that would rival those of Chartres or Cologne. It did not materialise.'

56 CHRISTINE DE LUCA, a Shetlander living in Edinburgh, has published four volumes of poetry, most recently *Parallel Worlds* (2005). Hansel Cooperative Press has published her poetry in pamphlet form and her children's stories – book and CDs – in Shetland dialect. She is chair of Shore Poets in Edinburgh. For more information, see www.christinedeluca.co.uk. The inspiration for this poem was a brooch found by her grandfather while fishing and given to her mother. Since lost again!

57 **DIANA HENDRY** has published three poetry collections, *Making Blue, Borderers* and *Twelve Lilts: Psalms and Responses,* plus *Sparks!* with Tom Pow. Her nearly forty children's books include *No Homework Tomorrow: Poems, Harvey Angell* (Whitbread Award 1991) and *You Can't Kiss it Better.* She has worked as a journalist, a creative writing tutor and as Writer in Residence at Dumfries & Galloway Royal Infirmary. She lives in Edinburgh. The 'Bidie-in' poems marked the beginning of a personal and professional partnership with Hamish Whyte.

58 **HAMISH WHYTE**, born near Glasgow where he lived until moving to Edinburgh in 2004, has published several poetry pamphlets, including *Apple on an Orange Day* and *Christmasses;* edited many anthologies, including *Noise and Smoky Breath: an Illustrated Anthology of Glasgow Poems, The Scottish Cat* and *An Arran Anthology,* and co-edited many issues of *New Writing Scotland.* He runs Mariscat Press, publishing poetry, has worked as a librarian and is an Honorary Research Fellow in the Scottish Literature Department, University of Glasgow. The 'Bidie-in' poems marked the beginning of a personal and professional partnership with Diana Hendry.

59 **ANON** 'The Twa Corbies' There are many forms of this, one of the most concise and best-known of the Ballads. Certainly none expresses our condition of mortality more succinctly and chillingly than this overheard dualogue, with its mixture of bleak beauty and fatalism, braided with sardonic glee.

60 **ANDREW GREIG** was born in Bannockburn, Stirling. Now a fulltime writer, he lives in Orkney and the Scottish Borders. He has published five novels including *In Another Light*, six collections of poetry of which the most recent is *Into You* (2001), two mountaineering books chronicling his Himalayan expeditions, and *Preferred Lies*, about life, mortality, golf and Scotland. This poem was first drafted, near complete, in pencil on the flyleaf of *A Gradual Awakening* by Stephen Levine, some months after his leaving Intensive Care.

61 **IAN MCDONOUGH** lives in Edinburgh with his partner and daughter. His poem sequence *A Rising Fever* was published in 2000, in which year he was commissioned by the Engineering and Science Research Council and Strathclyde University to produce a series of poems on particle physics. His first full-length poetry collection was *Clan MacHine* (2002). 'A Night in Stoer Lighthouse' emerged almost fully-formed after a dream-sodden night spent there.

62 **GEORGE CAMPBELL HAY** grew up in Kintyre, attending school in Edinburgh and university in Oxford. During the war he spent time in North Africa and Italy, before being transferred to Greece, where a violent incident led to the onset of a mental illness which would dog him for the remainder of his life. A prolific linguist and translator, his poems are principally in Gaelic, but he also wrote in Scots, English, Italian, French, Danish and other languages. His *Collected Poems and Songs* were published posthumously in 2000.

63 **EDWIN MUIR** was born in Deerness and brought up on Wyre, in Orkney, but moved to Glasgow with his family when he was fourteen. His vision was dominated by a longing for lost Edens and (as in the poem here) childhood, and an apocalyptic sense of war and its aftermath. Also an influential critic, from 1921 on he travelled in Europe, and in the 1930s assisted his wife

Willa to translate Kafka. In the 1950s he was Warden of Newbattle Abbey College, then Visiting Professor of Poetry at Harvard. His seven individual volumes of poetry are collected in *The Complete Poems of Edwin Muir* (1991).

64 **ROBERT RENDALL**'s publications included *Orkney Variants* and other volumes of poems, represented in *An Island Shore: The Life and Work of Robert Rendall* (1990); religious works, and a memoir *Orkney Shore*. Of his lyrics in the Orkney dialect, which he saw as 'a thin survival from the speech of the ancient Norse earldom, diluted by Scots' idioms and vocabulary, and now heard only in a context of common English', George Mackay Brown wrote, 'No future anthology of Scottish Poetry dare ignore these perfectly wrought pieces'.

65 **ALAN SPENCE** is a poet and playwright, novelist and short-story writer. He is based in Edinburgh, where he and his wife run the Sri Chinmoy meditation centre. He is also Professor in Creative Writing at the University of Aberdeen where he is Artistic Director of the annual WORD Festival. He writes: '"Song" sang itself into my head one fine clear evening in Glencoe. It's a matter of some pride that it was once adopted by a school in the East End of Glasgow as their school song (sung to the tune of *The Red Flag*!).'

66 **ANON** 'All Wemen are Guid: equivocal verses' This curio is taken from the Maitland MS of 1568, compiled by Sir Richard Maitland of Lethington (1496– 1586), a legal judge and himself a poet. Its meaning – and its attitude towards women – varies radically in keeping with where the breath pauses are placed.

67 **JIM C. WILSON** lives in East Lothian. He has taught Poetry in Practice sessions at Edinburgh University

since 1994, and has been a Royal Literary Fund Fellow since 2001. His poem was inspired by a poster he encountered in a renovated mill in rural Andalucía. Every day he stared at the picture of the blue and yellow room, until he began to wonder what it would be like to inhabit such a place. Eventually postcard copies of the 1946 Matisse painting were tracked down – in St Andrews.

68 **JAMES MCGONIGAL** was born in Dumfries. He combines writing with teaching, educational research and academic editorial work. He has published poetry and prose for adults and children (in both English and Scots), and co-edited several anthologies of contemporary writing. Some of his poetry and translations are collected in *Driven Home* (1998) and in the long poem *Passage/An Pasaiste* (2004). 'The Eye of the Beholder' recounts what helps to sustain him in the midst of things.

69 **WILLIAM DUNBAR** was born in East Lothian. Evidence is that he graduated from St Andrews University in 1479, and trained as a Franciscan novice, travelling to England and Picardy before leaving the order. He served, initially in an ambassadorial role, at the court of James IV; but his latter years, and death, remain a mystery. Central to the 'Golden Age' of Scottish literature, he had the most dazzling range and technical virtuosity of all the mediaeval *makars*. In contrast to his penchant for noble eulogy, the aureate richness and exuberance of 'The Thrissill and the Rois', and the scurrilous invective and muscularity of his flytings and satires on the church, this bejewelled miniature depicts his exquisite but merciless lady firstly *in* then as the 'garth' or garden.

70 JAMES GRAHAM, MARQUIS OF MONTROSE Though one of the first to sign the Covenant in 1638, he fought for Charles I in the Civil War, prior to his defeat at Philiphaugh. After a spell in Europe, and an attempt to raise soldiers for Charles II, he was executed in Edinburgh. Whilst employing the terminology of love verses, this poem was in fact written as his political testament.

71 JACKIE KAY grew up in Glasgow and lives in Manchester with her son. She teaches creative writing at Newcastle University. Her novel *Trumpet* won the Guardian Fiction Award. She has written two collections of short stories, *Why Don't You Stop Talking* (2002) and *Wish I was Here* (2006). Her collection of poems *Life Mask* (2005) draws on the experience of having her head sculpted for a series of poets' herms in an Edinburgh business park. She is a fellow of The Royal Society of Literature and Lead Advisor to the Literature Department at The Arts Council of Great Britain.

72 SHEENA BLACKHALL is a North East writer, storyteller, traditional singer and illustrator born in Aberdeen and brought up on Deeside. From 1998 to 2003 she was Creative Writing Fellow in Scots at Aberdeen University's Elphinstone Institute. She has had 47 poetry pamphlets, 10 short story collections and two novellas published. 'The Spik o' the Lan' comes from an early volume. A Western Buddhist, she adheres to the Perennial Philosophy 'All in one, One in all...'. The poem states this very simply, in Scots.

73 JOHN BURNSIDE was born in Dunfermline and lives in East Fife. He is Reader in Creative Writing at the University of St Andrews. His nine collections of poetry include *The Myth of the Twin* (1994), *The Asylum Dance*

(2000), *The Light Trap* (2002) and most recently *The Good Neighbour* (2005). He has also published five books of fiction. His *Selected Poems* were published in 2006, as was his memoir *A Lie About My Father.*

74 **HUGH MacDIARMID** (C.M. Grieve) was born in Langholm and after war service settled in Montrose as a journalist, with his *Scottish Chapbook* (1922–23) promoting the Scots language. Scotland's most influential and controversial writer of the 20th century, he urged the regeneration of all aspects of Scottish literature and culture. *A Drunk Man Looks at the Thistle* (1926), with its synthesis of Braid or Lowland Scots and other sources, is generally cited as the masterwork of modern Scottish poetry. In 1928 he was a founding member of the National Party of Scotland. His *Collected Poems* and many volumes of prose have been published over the past decade. 'The Watergaw', from *Sangshaw* (1925), uncannily links the rainbow to the expression on the face of a dying friend.

75 **CAROL ANN DUFFY** was born in Glasgow. Educated at St Joseph's Convent, Stafford and Liverpool University, she lives in Manchester with her daughter. She has written for both children and adults. Poetry collections include *Standing Female Nude* (1985), *Selling Manhattan* (1987), *Meantime* (1993), *The World's Wife* (1999), *Feminine Gospels* (2002) and *New Selected Poems 1984–2004*. The latest, *Rapture* (2006), won the T.S. Eliot Prize.

76 **DILYS ROSE** lives in Edinburgh. She has published ten books of fiction and poetry, the most recent being *Lure, Lord of Illusions* and *Selected Stories* (all 2005). In progress are 'Bodyworks' (poems) and a libretto, 'The Child of Europe'. Over a period of several years the

Rose/McCabe family regularly visited a house in Perth which had a separate, narrow staircase leading to what would originally have been the maid's room. This became a great source of melodrama to their girls who, she says, would construct horror-movie scenarios – filmed with camcorder – and insist on escorting visitors up the stairs by candle or torchlight.

77 **RICHARD PRICE** grew up in Renfrewshire and studied at Napier College and at the University of Strathclyde, where he combined English studies with Librarianship. His PhD thesis was on the overcoming of tragedy in the novels of Neil Gunn. His work is essentially that of a love poet who uses the materials of the contemporary world lyrically. 'The world is busy, Katie' was an attempt, in his own words, 'to soothe my daughter to sleep with a poem, and to find another rhythm inside the formal sonnet that maybe added a kind of syncopation within its, to me, elongated basic line'.

78 **HELENA NELSON** is both poet and critic, reviewing poetry as well as running HappenStance Press (www.happenstancepress.com) and editing *Sphinx*, a magazine dedicated to chapbook poetry. 'Cake' featured first in *Mr and Mrs Philpott on Holiday in Auchterawe & Other Poems* (2001), and later in *Starlight on Water* (2003). The on-going Philpott sequence, and 'Cake' in particular, are 'about the sort of love which thrives in difficult circumstances in later life. The curious thing about an excellent cake is that the better it is, the sooner it vanishes…'.

79 **ADAM MCNAUGHTAN** grew up in Dennistoun, in Glasgow. His involvement with the Scottish Folk Revival, during which he gained prominence, stems from the 1950s. Over the decades since, he has gained

international recognition as an influential writer, collector, researcher and singer of songs, among them his own wittily and hilariously compressed 'Oor Hamlet'. The song by which he is represented here is much anthologised.

80 **MARGARET HAMILTON** was born in Glasgow. Her poetry, short stories and a novel *Bull's Penny* employed west of Scotland dialect to reproduce the spoken language of ordinary people. 'Lament for a Lost Dinner Ticket', which appeared first in *Scottish International* and has since been anthologised, is notable for the wit of its transcription and shift from the child's delivery to her version of adult speech.

81 **DONNY O'ROURKE**, from Glasgow, sees the four points of his saltire as poetry, journalism, broadcasting and university teaching. A graduate of the universities of Glasgow and Cambridge, he divides his year between his Glasgow base and scholarly wanderings to Germany, Pembroke College Cambridge and New Mexico. 'The events recorded in "Milk" happened just as the poem says they did; and the sentiments are as authentically, or fraudulently simple as they seem. Most writers concoct the necessary myth, and Mum's Antrim, my Dalriada, is an enormous part of the founding fable that sustains me as a doubt deeved poet and person.'

82 **JOSEPH LEE** was an artist, poet and journalist born in Dundee, the inspiration for a first book of poem, *Tales o' our Town* (1910). A Black Watch sergeant in the Great War, he sent home poems and sketches describing fighting in the trenches; and published *A Captive at Carlsruhe*, on his experiences as a prisoner-of-war. His poems appeared alongside those of Sassoon, Owen and others, but were later ignored. After the Second

World War he moved to London. In 1944 he and his wife returned to Dundee, where he died in 1949.

83 **SORLEY MacLEAN** / *Somhairle MacGill-Eain* was born on the island of Raasay. Schooled on Skye, he studied English at Edinburgh University. He served with the Signals Corps in North Africa during the Second World, being wounded at El Alamein. His first book, *Dàin do Eimhir agus Dàin Eile*, was published by William MacLellan in 1943: a new edition (ASLS, 2002) includes some hitherto uncollected poems from the series. He received the Queen's Gold Medal for Poetry in 1990, and his most recent *Collected* edition was published by Carcanet/Birlinn in 1999. With eerie beauty, 'Hallaig' invokes a Raasay township where his ancestors lived, before the Clearances.

84 **KATE CLANCHY** was born in Glasgow, and grew up there and in Edinburgh. This is one of her very earliest poems, and comes from her first collection, *Slattern* (1996). She has since published two others, *Samarkand* (1999) and *Newborn* (2004). She lives in Oxford with her family and works as a teacher, broadcaster and freelance writer.

85 **ANON** 'The Two Sisters' This ballad has a number of variants, as has its refrain, the one here being perhaps a corruption of the common burden 'Hey Nunny, Nunny'. The breathtaking presence, and entrance-ment, of the clàrsach playing on its own are thought to have been added by Walter Scott.

86 **TOM POW**, from Edinburgh, lives in Dumfries where he teaches creative writing and storytelling at Glasgow University's Crichton Campus. Besides four full collec-tions of poetry, including *Landscapes and Elegies* (2004),

he has written radio drama, a travel book, and picture books and novels for young adults. 'Crabs: Tiree' is a holiday memory: 'I knew all I had to do was describe the incident as clearly as I could. I've become more aware of the narrative aspect of my work since I began to teach storytelling. And I know that it's best to let the story/poem do its work as a metaphor with no further comment from me.'

87 **BRIAN JOHNSTONE**'s poetry publications include *The Lizard Silence* (1996) and *Homing* (2004). His work has appeared in journals and anthologies throughout the UK, as well as in America and a number of European countries. His poems 'evoke... a sense of spiritual immanence in their slow still spaces' (*Scottish Literary Journal*); and have been translated into Catalan, Swedish, Polish and Lithuanian. He lives in Fife and is Festival Director of StAnza, Scotland's Poetry Festival.

88 **ANON** 'The Bewteis of the Fute-Ball' This quatrain appears in the Bannatyne Manuscript, the treasure-chest of mediaeval Scots poetry collected and tran-scribed by an Edinburgh merchant, George Bannatyne, on his return to Forfar in 1568, to avoid the Plague. The Court accounts for 11 April 1497 note a sum 'giffin to Jame Dog to by fut ballis to the King', James IV.

89 **JOHN GLENDAY** is the author of two collections, *The Apple Ghost* (1989) and *Undark* (1995). In 1990–91 he was appointed Scottish/Canadian Exchange Fellow, based at the University of Alberta and in 2000–2001 he was Associate Writer at Edinburgh University's Centre for Lifelong Learning. 'Once Upon a Time' was 'one of those poems that festered for a long time... then suddenly fell into reasonable shape with little

conscious effort – a bit like a jug of milk unbreaking itself'.

90 **ALISON FLETT** was born and bred in Edinburgh but has been living in Orkney for the past seven years. The poem 'Lernin' is published in her collection *Whit Lassyz Ur Inty* (2004) and was written after witnessing an incident in the St James Shopping Centre, Edinburgh. She is currently working on a book of short stories.

91 **HAMISH HENDERSON** was born in Blairgowrie, Perthshire and attended Dulwich College and Cambridge University. A poet, songwriter and folklorist, during the Second World War he served as an intelligence officer with the Highland Division in North Africa. From 1951 until his death he was the School of Scottish Studies of Edinburgh University's foremost field researcher, discovering and collecting traditional songs, and a leading figure in the Scottish folk revival. His war experience is reflected in *Elegies for the Dead in Cyrenaica* (1948), and *Collected Poems and Songs* was published in 2000.

92 **JAMES HOGG**, born and raised on a farm in the Ettrick Forest, came to Edinburgh in 1810. He returned in his later years to farm in Yarrow. A lifelong friend of Walter Scott, his literary output straddles *The Private Memoirs and Confessions of a Justified Sinner* (the psychological novel regarded as his masterpiece), stories, a poem sequence *The Queen's Wake* and a pastoral verse fantasy, *Kilmeny*. In *The Mountain Bard* (1807) he avows the influence of this 'beautiful old rhyme which I have often heard my mother repeat'. The imagery of the earliest known (15th century) English version, thought to stem from some form of the Grail legend, is supplanted here by something more akin to Border balladry.

93 **KATHLEEN JAMIE** was born in the west of Scotland. Her poetry collections include *Jizzen* (1999), *Mr and Mrs Scotland are Dead* (2002) and *The Tree House* (2004). Of her non-fiction books, *Among Muslims* (2002) recounts her travels in Northern Pakistan, and *Findings* (2005) her travels in Scotland and discoveries in the natural world. A part-time Reader in Creative Writing at St Andrews University, Kathleen Jamie lives with her family in Fife.

94 **GEORGE BRUCE** was born and brought up in Fraserburgh, and educated at Aberdeen University. For three decades he was a radio producer with the BBC, latterly in Edinburgh. The landscape and sea of the North-East, and his own genealogy, are interwoven in his sparse early poems. 'Departure and Departure and...' opens *Pursuit, Poems 1986–1998*, dedicated to the memory of his wife. A collected volume *Today Tomorrow* appeared in 2001, and *Through the Letterbox*, with illustrations by Elizabeth Blackadder, in 2003.

95 **LEWIS SPENCE** was born in Broughty Ferry, Dundee, and studied dentistry before turning to writing. His range of interests and expertise is reflected in his *Dictionary of Mythology* and *Encyclopaedia of Occultism*. He was one of the founders of the Scottish National Party in 1928. His poems appeared in *The Phoenix* and *Weirds and Vanities*, and in his *Collected Poems* of 1953. He drew flamboyantly, as in this piece in the old high-ballad style, on archaic Scots.

96 **ANGUS CALDER**, while Staff Tutor in Arts for the Open University in Scotland, was Convener of the Scottish Poetry Library on its founding. Best known as an historian, he began to publish poetry regularly in his fifties, his collections including *Waking in Waikato* (1997) and *Sun Behind the Castle* (2004). He lives in Tollcross, Edinburgh, as a freelance writer. He recalls: 'I began to compose this poem on the bus from Haymarket to Murrayfield and produced a full draft (later little changed) before my match. I relish the fact that the wonderful sport of curling can feature in verses which non-curlers seem to like.'

97 **ALEXANDER HUME** After some years at the court of James VI, and tired of seeking royal favour, Hume turned in 1598 to the Church. Becoming minister of Logie, near Stirling, he renounced his earlier secular writings. The stanzas here conclude one of the finest and most exquisite of Scots nature poems, tempered by his spirituality.

98 **NORMAN KREITMAN**, now retired from medical research, lives in Edinburgh. He has published three collections of poetry (*Touching Rock, Against Leviathan* and *Casanova's 72nd Birthday*) as well as studies of poetic imagery (*The Roots of Metaphor*) and allied topics. He also greatly enjoys fishing, and this recent poem reflects his constant astonishment at the optimism of fellow anglers.

99 **ROBERT LOUIS STEVENSON** was born in Edinburgh, his father a lighthouse engineer. He studied engineering but switched to law, becoming an advocate in 1875. His heart, however, was in writing. Early travel and adventure tales led to a wide range of stylistically impeccable essays, stories, and novels including *Treasure Island* and *Kidnapped*. His poems were collected in *A Child's Garden of Verses* and *Underwoods*. Always frail, he left Britain with his wife Fanny Osborne, for the sake of his health. They settled in the South Seas where

he died aged 44. This late poem, touchingly fusing a sense of exile and of his own mortality, appeared in the *Pall Mall Gazette* as 'Home Thoughts from Samoa'.

100 **NANCY SOMERVILLE**, a Glaswegian by birth, lives and works in Edinburgh. In 2004 she co-edited *Goldfish Suppers*, a collection of poems and illustrations commissioned for families with young children. She is a member of Shore Poets: www.shorepoets.org.uk and Diggers Writers: www.yonkly.co.uk. 'The Big Hooley', part of a sequence '1st July 1999', commenting on the first day of the new Scottish Parliament, also appeared in the anthology *Edinburgh: An Intimate City* (2000).

Luath Press Limited
committed to publishing well written books worth reading

LUATH PRESS takes its name from Robert Burns, whose little collie Luath (*Gael.*, swift or nimble) tripped up Jean Armour at a wedding and gave him the chance to speak to the woman who was to be his wife and the abiding love of his life. Burns called one of *The Twa Dogs* Luath after Cuchullin's hunting dog in Ossian's *Fingal*. Luath Press was established in 1981 in the heart of Burns country, and is now based a few steps up the road from Burns' first lodgings on Edinburgh's Royal Mile.

Luath offers you distinctive writing with a hint of unexpected pleasures.

Most bookshops in the UK, the US, Canada, Australia, New Zealand and parts of Europe either carry our books in stock or can order them for you. To order direct from us, please send a £sterling cheque, postal order, international money order or your credit card details (number, address of cardholder and expiry date) to us at the address below. Please add post and packing as follows: UK – £1.00 per delivery address; overseas surface mail – £2.50 per delivery address; overseas airmail – £3.50 for the first book to each delivery address, plus £1.00 for each additional book by airmail to the same address. If your order is a gift, we will happily enclose your card or message at no extra charge.

Luath Press Limited
543/2 Castlehill
The Royal Mile
Edinburgh EH1 2ND
Scotland
Telephone: 0131 225 4326 (24 hours)
Fax: 0131 225 4324
Email: sales@luath.co.uk
Website: www.luath.co.uk